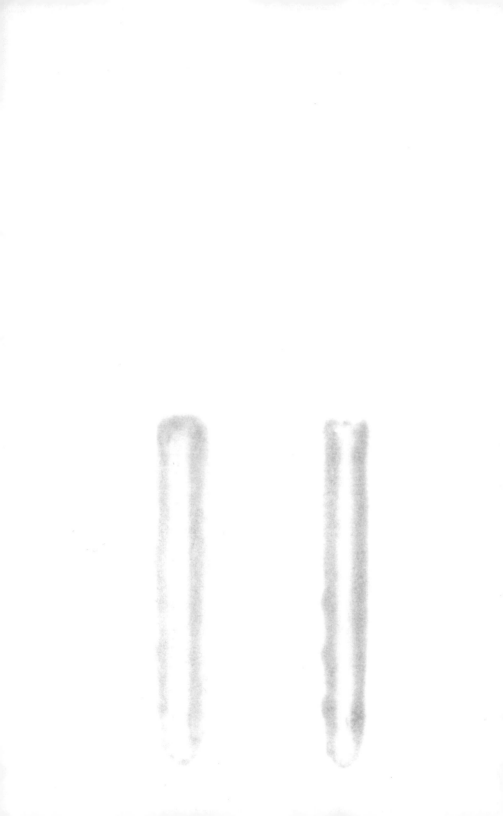

Angus Wilson

Twayne's English Authors Series

Kinley E. Roby, Editor

Northeastern University

TEAS 401

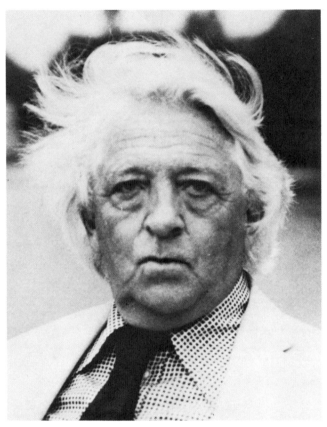

ANGUS WILSON
*Photograph by, and
courtesy of, Tony Garrett*

Angus Wilson

By Averil Gardner

Memorial University of Newfoundland

9560

Twayne Publishers • Boston

Angus Wilson

Averil Gardner

Copyright © 1985 by G.K. Hall & Company
All Rights Reserved
Published by Twayne Publishers
A Division of G. K. Hall & Co.
A publishing subsidiary of ITT
70 Lincoln Street
Boston, Massachusetts 02111

Book Production by Elizabeth Todesco
Book Design by Barbara Anderson

Printed on permanent/durable acid-free
paper and bound in the United States of America.

Library of Congress Cataloging in Publication Data

Gardner, Averil.
    Angus Wilson.

    (Twayne's English authors series; TEAS 401)
    Bibliography: p. 134
    Includes index.
    1. Wilson, Angus—Criticism and interpretation.
I. Title. II. Series.
PR 6045.I577Z67   1985   823'.914   84-23986
ISBN 0-8057-6891-2

Contents

About the Author
Preface
Chronology

Chapter One
Early Life and Times   1

Chapter Two
"Trifle Angus Wilson":
Two Volumes of Short Stories   12

Chapter Three
Distressed Liberals and Others   35

Chapter Four
Mid-Life Crises   57

Chapter Five
The Liberal at Armageddon   75

Chapter Six
Past and Present   86

Chapter Seven
Handing on the Torch   102

Chapter Eight
Ocelots and Jaguars   118

Notes and References   125
Selected Bibliography   134
Index   139

About the Author

Averil Gardner was born in 1937 in London, England. After reading English Language and Literature at the University of London, she taught in Japanese universities, including Tsuda Women's University near Tokyo, from 1961 to 1964. In 1964 she was appointed to the English Department of Memorial University of Newfoundland, Canada, where since 1976 she has been an Associate Professor of English. Her special areas of interest are Medieval Literature, Shakespeare, and the poetry and fiction of the nineteenth and twentieth centuries. She has published articles on medieval literature and on Oscar Wilde, in Japan, South Africa, and Canada. With Philip Gardner she is coauthor of *The God Approached: A Commentary on the Poems of William Empson* (Chatto & Windus, 1978).

Preface

Angus Wilson was the first important British writer of fiction to make his debut after the end of World War II. With the publication in 1949 of his volume of short stories, *The Wrong Set,* he was immediately recognized as an interpreter of British life and behavior of uncommon sensitivity. In the more than thirty years since then, he has consolidated a reputation of the greatest distinction, blending in eight substantial novels a traditional and liberal concern with character, manners, and morals with an ever-renewed alertness to the changing world and to new modes of fictional presentation.

The broad range of Wilson's contribution to literature entitles him not simply to the appellation of "writer" but to that of "man of letters." His achievements as a writer of fiction are so substantial as to have caused the present study to focus almost exclusively on them; but in addition to his creative work Wilson has extensively reviewed the literary work of others, particularly in three highly praised critical-biographical volumes on writers he greatly admires: Emile Zola, Charles Dickens, Rudyard Kipling. He has also found time and energy to lecture on literature in England, Europe, the United States, Canada, and Australia; and his roles in the literary world of postwar Britain, after more than a decade spent in the service of the British Museum library, have included the Chairmanship of the National Book League and of the Literature Panel of the Arts Council. Rarely has one man made so diverse and influential a contribution to the world of letters. He was knighted in 1980.

Three previous books devoted solely to Wilson's work have appeared in England, between 1964 and 1980. Though all of these are of value, none of them, inevitably, deals with all of Wilson's work. The present study is the first to be published in the United States, a country which Wilson has often visited and in which (at the University of Iowa) most of his manuscripts have found a home. No doubt, like previous studies, it is destined to be rendered incomplete by future publications by Wilson; but it has tried to keep pace with his fiction to date, and includes a consideration of his latest novel (1980), *Setting the World on Fire.*

I am glad to acknowledge assistance received from many quarters in the preparation of this book. Sir Angus Wilson kindly allowed me to interview him in Cambridge, and was a generous host at his home, Felsham Woodside in Suffolk; he also checked the accuracy of my first (biographical) chapter. I am much indebted to him. I am also indebted to Mr. Tony Garrett for his assistance, and particularly for his fine photograph of Sir Angus, which serves as the frontispiece of this book. The Memorial University of Newfoundland awarded me a grant to enable me to do research for my book in Cambridge, England, and at the University of Iowa. At the former, I was greatly assisted by the staffs of the Reading Room, Periodicals Room, and Rare Books Room of the University Library; at the latter, Professor Frederick MacDowell generously smoothed my path and Mr. Frank Paluka, Head of Special Collections, and Ms. Vevalee Voots made my work with the Angus Wilson manuscripts a pleasure. Mrs. Cathy Murphy, Departmental Secretary, willingly typed and retyped my manuscript. My husband and colleague, Philip Gardner, has given me constant help and support during the preparation of this book.

I am grateful to Sir Angus Wilson for allowing me to quote from his work, and to the following publishers of his work: to William Morrow & Co. Inc. for *The Wrong Set* and *Such Darling Dodos;* to the University of California Press for *The Wild Garden;* to Viking Penguin Inc. for *Hemlock and After, Late Call, No Laughing Matter,* and *Setting the World on Fire.* I am also indebted to the *New Statesman* and Ms. June Mercer for allowing me to quote "Trifle Angus Wilson"; and to Weidenfeld and Nicolson for a passage from *The Letters of Evelyn Waugh* (ed. Mark Amory).

Averil Gardner

Memorial University of Newfoundland

Chronology

1913	Angus Wilson born at Bexhill, Sussex, the youngest of six brothers.
1920–1924	Lives in Durban, South Africa, with his mother's relatives.
1924–1927	Attends a preparatory school in Seaford, Sussex, run by his second-eldest brother.
1927–1932	Attends Westminster School as a day boy, while living with his parents in various London hotels.
1929	Death of Wilson's mother.
1932–1935	Reads medieval history at Merton College, Oxford.
1936	Obtains post at the British Museum, London (now the British Library).
1938	Death of Wilson's father.
1941–1944	Works for Foreign Office Intelligence at their establishment at Bletchley Park, Buckinghamshire.
1946–1955	At British Museum (from 1949 as Deputy Superintendent of the Reading Room).
1949	*The Wrong Set* published.
1950	*Such Darling Dodos.*
1952	*Emile Zola,* February. *Hemlock and After,* July.
1953	*For Whom the Cloche Tolls.*
1955	Resigns from the British Museum. Keeps a flat in Dolphin Square, Pimlico, but also acquires a cottage at Felsham Woodside, Bradfield St. George, Suffolk, where he has continued to live. *The Mulberry Bush* first performed by the Bristol Old Vic Company, 27 September.
1956	*The Mulberry Bush* published, February; also performed at the Royal Court Theatre, London, 2 April. *Anglo-Saxon Attitudes,* May. Book Society Fiction choice.

1957   *A Bit off the Map. The Mulberry Bush* televised. Attends (with Stephen Spender) P.E.N. Conference in Japan.

1958   *The Middle Age of Mrs. Eliot,* August. (Awarded the James Tait Black Prize.) Fellow of the Royal Society of Literature.

1960   Ewing Lecturer, University of California, Los Angeles, October. Moody Lecturer, University of Chicago.

1961   Gives Northcliffe Lectures ("Evil in the English Novel"), University of London. *The Old Men at the Zoo,* September.

1963   *The Wild Garden* (expansion of the Ewing Lectures). Play, "The Invasion", televised. Joins faculty of the University of East Anglia (part-time).

1964   *Tempo: The Impact of Television on the Arts. Late Call.* Attends (with William Golding) Leningrad Writers' Congress.

1966   Appointed Professor of English Literature (part-time), University of East Anglia (retired 1973). Chairman of the Literature Panel, Arts Council of Great Britain. Participates in Adelaide Festival of the Arts, Australia.

1967   Beckeman Professor, University of California, Berkeley. *No Laughing Matter.*

1968   Appointed C.B.E. Honorary Fellow, Cowell College, University of California, Santa Cruz.

1970   *The World of Charles Dickens.*

1971–1974   Chairman of the National Book League.

1972   Companion of Literature. Chevalier de l'Ordre des Arts et des Lettres.

1973   *As If by Magic.*

1974   John Hinkley Visiting Professor, Johns Hopkins University. *Late Call* televised.

1976   *The Strange Ride of Rudyard Kipling.*

1980   *Setting the World on Fire.* Awarded a knighthood.

Chapter One
Early Life and Times

Angus Wilson is unusual among twentieth-century British writers in at least two ways. He seems, in the first place, never to have served a literary apprenticeship or to have experienced any difficulty in getting his first work published. He speaks of having contributed pieces to the school magazine of his preparatory school, and one short story to *The Elizabethan,* the school magazine of his public school, Westminster,[1] but, apart from these juvenilia, Angus Wilson wrote nothing until the age of thirty-three, when in a single Sunday in November 1946 he produced his short story, "Raspberry Jam." Together with eleven other stories written in rapid succession on subsequent weekends,[2] this was published in 1949 in his first collection, *The Wrong Set.* Only three of these stories had previously appeared in print, but these came out in excellent magazines: "Realpolitik" in *The Listener,* "Mother's Sense of Fun" and "Crazy Crowd" in Cyril Connolly's *Horizon.* Such prestigious first appearances, coupled with the willingness of an important firm, Secker and Warburg, to bring out as part of a collection nine stories not previously published, is impressive testimony to the power of Wilson's late-flowering talent, and to the authority with which he was able to handle material drawn from the experiences, opinions, and emotions of his earlier life. The confidence placed in Wilson's work by his publishers was soon repaid by favorable public, as well as critical, interest: Peter Faulkner has stated that the first impression of *The Wrong Set* was sold out in two weeks.[3]

Since 1949 and his emergence fully armed on the literary scene as a writer of short stories, Angus Wilson has become one of Britain's most important postwar novelists, and the degree of public recognition his career has brought him constitutes his second claim to unusualness among his fellow writers. His third novel, *The Middle Age of Mrs. Eliot,* won him in 1958 both the James Tait Black Memorial Prize and the French Prize for the Best Foreign Novel; in the same year he was made a Fellow of the Royal Society of Literature. The latter distinction, not itself remarkable for an important writer, at least conveys the esteem in which Wilson is held by his literary peers. What is more notable is the sequence of honors that have come in the last two decades. In 1968 Wilson was made Companion of the Order of the British Empire; in 1972, Companion of Literature and also Chevalier of the French Order of Arts and Letters. Most recently, in 1980, he was awarded a knighthood, a comparatively rare honor for a novelist. It would of course be naive to measure the stature of a writer entirely in terms of public honors; but in Wilson's case their quantity and quality suggest the ability of his writing to communicate with a wide spectrum of readers and accurately reflect its panoramic range and its abiding concern with human values and human beings.

Formation of a Writer

In his entry in *Who's Who* Angus Wilson lists his recreations as "gardening, travel," so revealing in the simplest form the sense of contrast on which his view of the world is based. The cultivation of a garden implies rootedness, or at least usually involves being settled in a particular place, and since the mid-1950s Wilson has lived in a small village in Suffolk, near Bury St. Edmunds. But he has also traveled widely, particularly in the Far East and the United States, and in *The Wild Garden* (1963), a book derived from lectures he gave there in 1960, he has said: "I shudder at the idea of 'being settled.' "[4] His most recent novel, *Setting the World on Fire* (1980), presents two brothers whose instinctive attitudes to life externalize a similar dichotomy in Wilson himself: a creative urge to take risks, to make a splash, is represented by Piers Mosson, a more cautious wish for order and organization is represented by his brother Tom. Throughout the whole of Wilson's fiction may be discerned a fruitful tension between traditionalism—in the form of long, neo-Victorian novels of "character"—and the urge to experiment, displayed for instance in the unnerving future-visions of *The Old Men at the Zoo* (1961) and the use of dramatic interludes in *No Laughing Matter* (1967).

"At the very heart of my symbolic view of life," Wilson says in *The Wild Garden* (*WG*, 61), is the dichotomy between Town and Country, between two kinds of garden which are yet, as he admits, the same thing seen from different angles: the "wild garden" which simulates the disorder of nature in an orderly way, and the "garden or clearing in the wild" which demonstrates man's ability to conquer that powerful disorder but only within narrow limits. The two images are related by Wilson to the different characters and backgrounds of his parents, who occur in various guises in his work, and one may say that if his leanings toward order and rootedness are a reaction against the unsettled quality of his life with them, his impulse towards travel, movement, and change are equally the product of it. Certainly, the family and its relationships possess an unusual importance for him as a writer.

Angus Frank Johnstone Wilson was born in August 1913 in Sussex, in the small and rather genteel seaside resort of Bexhill, located between the larger seaside resorts of Hastings and Eastbourne. His father was forty-eight years old when Wilson was born, his mother forty-four, and as he was the youngest of six brothers the nearest of whom to him was thirteen years older, his upbringing was in effect that of an only child of middle-aged parents. He has described himself as at this time "a very spoilt, frightened, untruthful child,"[5] and from his story "Necessity's Child," published in *Such Darling Dodos* (1950), it is clear that he was often lonely as well. During World War I, when he alternated "summer mornings on the beach . . . with afternoons catching butterflies or grasshoppers in the lush meadowland that surrounded my father's tennis-club" (*WG,* 91–92), three of his brothers were involved in fighting on the other side of the English Channel, and his mother's anxiety for their welfare, communicated to her young son, created in him a fear of the sea. Parental anxiety was accompanied by patriotic bigotry. Wilson's parents were blindly anti-German: his father unquestioningly credited stories of German atrocities and condoned harsh Australian reprisals, and his mother, when Wilson was about five, "ordered my twice-wounded brother out of the house because he expressed doubts about German barbarity."[6]

The Wilson family milieu was plainly not an intellectual one; in fact, though he seems to have liked it no less for this, it was "often a household of shouts, screams, kicking, and objects hurtling through the air" (*WG,* 69)—an atmosphere matched by the sometimes hyperactive texture of Wilson's own fictional prose. When in the mood to be fashionably dismissive of his family, as he was in his "1930s progressive" phase, Wilson called it "lumpen-bourgeois."[7] But although they partook of that now-rare middle-class attitude that exalted public school education and attached no particular value to universities, Wilson's parents, at least in their combined origins and early experiences, were rather more than ordinary middle-class people, and it was from their talkative habit of "compensation for lost glories by means of fantasy" that Wilson "early imbibed a fiction-making atmosphere" (*WG*, 14). He learned also an admiration for the contrasted qualities of fatherly panache and motherly "pluck" which recur in many of his stories and novels, Arthur and Sylvia Calvert of *Late Call* being an example.

On his father's side Angus Wilson is of Lowland Scots extraction, which perhaps accounts for the strain of Calvinism that some critics have noticed in his work. His paternal grandfather, an officer in a good Scottish regiment, had a small estate in Dumfriesshire which was sublet into farms; on his way through London to help put down a rebellion in Canada, he met and married the daughter of a man reputed by Angus Wilson's siblings to have been either a diamond merchant or a publican, who lived in the 1860s in the Haymarket. It was here, in 1865, that Angus Wilson's father, William Johnstone-Wilson, was born, though he was later brought up in Dumfriesshire in a Regency or early Victorian house set in an area of "small lochs and downland and salmon rivers" (*WG*, 73) which his son visited with him for the first time in 1929.

William Johnstone-Wilson was far from being the Calvinist in his own behavior, being given in his later life to gambling and a certain amount of marital infidelity. His upper-middle-class inheritance, before age twenty-one, of an income from the family estate left him with no need to work, and his son's account of him in *The Wild Garden* presents him as a throwback to the type of Regency buck: "He belonged to the eighteenth century stream that ran under the Victorian world and emerged as Edwardian" (*WG*, 69).

This "fascinating Englishman" (*WG*, 63) met his wife-to-be, Maude Caney, on a ship going to South Africa at the end of the 1880s. He, bored with reading for the bar, was in quest of adventure; she, a first-generation South African by birth, was returning to her parents' home in Durban after her first visit, in her late teens, to her grandfather in England. Her father, a well-to-do jeweler from Lincolnshire, had emigrated to South Africa in the 1850s, and his daughter had been brought up in a colonial society partly still pioneer in spirit—the Zulus annihilated the British at Isandhlwana, only 100 miles away, when she was ten—partly a genteel imitation of Victorian England. It was from her nostalgic accounts of her childhood in Natal that Angus Wilson formed his first idea of the "garden in the wild," just as he derived his image of the "wild garden" from his father's reminiscences of Dumfriesshire.

Wilson's parents were married in 1889. By the time he was born twenty-four years later their life was becoming one of "genteel poverty" (*WG,* 13) passed nomadically in a succession of houses, apartments, and small hotels, its disappointment soothed by embroidered recollections and sustained by the bourgeois ability to keep up appearances. The fascination, satiric yet compassionate, with the petty snobberies and stratagems of middle-class gentility, displayed particularly in Wilson's early work, clearly derives from his own childhood experience of them, gained first in a block of apartments in Bexhill, where his parents' friends were retired professional people older than themselves, and later in the London of the 1920s.

Between these two periods, however, Wilson experienced the world of his mother's girlhood at first hand, living in Durban between the ages of seven and eleven, and visiting the pineapple farm in neighboring Bellair that belonged to his ancient, blind great-uncle. Here he encountered his first mamba, as well as a sulphur-crested cockatoo and a green parrot (*WG,* 66). Many years later he recalled the effect on his imagination of his Durban life: "I remember how the snakes and rats beneath a South African house, built on stilts against the white ants, filled my dreams as a boy, for they had their own life, were only occasionally glimpsed yet were there."[8] Bellair seemed to him the "remote Jungle" and became, entangled with all his mother's earlier stories of it, an image of primeval happiness. But it was the social pleasures and family tensions of the visit, as they affected his mother, that Wilson transmuted into fiction, in the marvellously graphic detail of his story "Union Reunion," published in *The Wrong Set* in 1949.

By 1924 Wilson and his parents were back in England, they to the careful middle-class world of small hotels and "separate tables" in the Kensington area of London, he to a preparatory school at Seaford near Newhaven in Sussex, run by his second-eldest brother. At his brother's school Wilson was not a dazzling pupil academically. Rather he was lively and "sophisticated," persuading the dancing mistress to teach the boys the Charleston,[9] and involved in school productions of Gilbert and Sullivan operas, in which he was reckoned a superb actor if not a good singer. He also organized acting "games" based on historical novels such as Baroness Orczy's *The Scarlet Pimpernel,* in which he took all the best parts himself.

While at Seaford he visited the two British Empire exhibitions held at Wembley in 1924 and 1925. There he noticed how the "unvocal imperial sentiment" of his headmaster-brother and the "euphoric imperialism" of his mother were alike "nonplussed by what they found there—a combination of a mammoth trade show and a large-scale fun fair."[10] One has not far to look for the origins of the sympathy with which, in many of his short stories, Wilson treats middle-class people displaced by the social changes that followed World War II: his own "Home and Colonial" family were clearly a vanishing breed well before that and indeed Wilson's mother, by then a "sad-eyed, embittered, courageous but snobbish Kensington woman" (WG, 63), died suddenly in the early spring of 1929 at the age of sixty. This event seems to have affected Wilson too deeply for him to have fictionalized it in his short stories other than indirectly, as for instance in "A Story of Historical Interest." Its effects remained with him for many years; one notes as recently as 1973, in As If By Magic, a passing reference to Hamo Langmuir's mother who died in a hotel[11]—a circumstance of his own mother's death which, demeaning as it was to her sense of propriety, Wilson strongly resented on her behalf in 1929 (WG, 51).

Before his mother died, Wilson had left preparatory school at Seaford and entered one of the oldest and most distinguished British public schools, Westminster. Despite his father's frequent tendency to outrun his own income and then make incursions into his wife's,[12] Wilson's parents managed to pay his fees as a day boy, so that he alternated between the stable environment of the school and the more uncertain one of the various hotels. He entered Westminster in 1927 and, despite previous qualms, found no bullying there but an atmosphere that was congenial and even a little dull. The headmaster at that time was Harold Costley-White, whose regime was described by one of his successors thus: "He devoted himself with unfailing energy to making Westminster a tolerant and civilised school."[13] It was so civilized that Wilson was able to avoid games by the simple expedient of signing his own name on the absence board, though later he took fencing. Having through the uncertainties of his childhood experienced a need to please others by entertaining them, he discovered at Westminster that his gift for "impressionistic mimicry"—which he later called his "principal natural asset as a writer" (WG, 16)—could be employed at the expense of the masters to amuse his schoolfellows. These were also struck by his odd appearance—small, dirty, with a shock of crimped yellow hair—and referred to him, without animus, as "the mad boy."[14] In his turn he told them outrageous and fanciful stories of his strange relatives, which resulted in some parents forbidding their sons to visit him in the holidays.[15] His histrionic talents found further outlet in his composition, with friends, of an un-written novel, scenes from which were acted out in the Army and Navy Stores in nearby Victoria Street, and, more officially, through taking part in school productions of drama and ballet.

The pleasures of his Westminster schooldays did not find a place in Wilson's fiction until some fifty years later, in his most recent novel, *Setting the World on Fire* (1980), but that very delay perhaps indicates their lasting effect on him, though Wilson's career at the school was neither so academically brilliant as that of Piers Mosson nor as academically assiduous as that of his brother Tom. But in his School Certificate year, though he acquired his necessary passes slowly, he did begin to discover the work of the great Russian nov-elists and of such moderns as Aldous Huxley and Evelyn Waugh, whose *Decline and Fall* and *Vile Bodies* "had just swept the sixth form off their feet."[16] Both had considerable influence on his own fiction later, and Evelyn Waugh in his turn became a great admirer of *Hem-lock and After* and *The Old Men at the Zoo*.

Among the Westminster masters, Wilson was particularly im-pressed by Laurie Tanner, the senior History master and keeper of the muniments of Westminster Abbey, who inculcated the virtues of de-corum and good sense. The Abbey itself, which serves as the school chapel, was something of a novelty to Wilson, indoctrinated as he had been by his mother, a Christian Scientist. Of greatest influence on Wilson, however, was a more dashing and more recent History master, John Edward Bowle, who told him to write novels, which he did not yet do, and encouraged him to specialize in History, which he did. He also introduced Wilson to a diet of Spengler, Croce, Freud, Gerald Heard, and Roger Fry, and gave him and other pupils more digestible meals at the Café Royal, Oscar Wilde's old haunt and unwittingly appropriate to Wilson who had already discovered in himself homosexual feelings and had had a number of "promiscuous sexual encounters . . . with cockney working-class young men."[17] Through Bowle, Wilson met brilliant young Oxford dons like John Sparrow and Maurice Bowra, and also Oscar Wilde's long-ago friend

Lord Alfred Douglas. The latter disappointed him by talking not about "the love that dares not speak its name" but about horse-racing—a particular addiction of Wilson's father.

Leaving Westminster in the summer of 1932, Angus Wilson went up to Oxford to read Medieval History. He was the first of his family to go to a university, and was only enabled to do so by the death of his mother: he had failed to obtain one of the closed scholarships to Christ Church available only to Westminster boys, but the portion of her capital that he inherited made it possible for him to take up a commoner's place at Merton College, where most of the undergraduates were less rich and fashionable. Over and above his fees and college expenses, he had in fact the ample sum of £300 a year to live on while at Oxford, and after some first-term fears that his "pansy" appearance and aesthetic tastes might expose him to "heaven knew what roastings and defenestrations" (MO, 96) at the hands of Merton's very small set of rich, drunken hearties, Wilson settled down to enjoying his time there. He was able to indulge a taste, learned from his father, for good food in restaurants, give small luncheon parties to his friends, and smoke a lot of expensive Turkish cigarettes; but he also read large numbers of great English novels, and plays, in the company of old schoolmates from Westminster, notably Daniel Pickering Walker, a French Scholar at Christ Church and now a Professor at the Warburg Institute of London University. (Wilson stayed with him in vacations, and dedicated Such Darling Dodos to his parents.) Through new friends at Merton, Wilson came to join an exclusive dining club called The Myrmidons, whose members wore "special violet evening coats and violet ties" (MO, 106); and acted in Shaw's The Doctor's Dilemma with the college Dramatic Society. He also figured in the more "gilded" Oxford represented by the University Dramatic Society (OUDS), playing in Marlowe's Doctor Faustus, and having his greatest success at a smoking concert where he represented one of the Seven Deadly Sins in a chorus, "wearing flame-colored pyjamas and carrying a madonna lily" (MO, 107). Something of the quality of his rather 'twenties—indeed even ninety-ish—life-style is suggested by the conclusion of his story 'Significant Experience,' the only fictional use Wilson has made of his Oxford years.

But Wilson's life at Oxford was not limited to pleasant, privileged self-indulgence, though of course this does accurately prefigure the delight in exuberance displayed by much of his fiction. He also got to know working-class students, whose industrial town backgrounds and staunch, firsthand Socialist beliefs gave solid reinforcement to the left-wing ideas that Wilson had picked up from some of the Westminster masters. One such student came from Manchester, another from the Black Country near Birmingham. With the latter Wilson attended Labour Club meetings in Oxford and took part in some demonstrations, but he found "most educative of all" the experience of "seeing Bilston, Darlaston and Wednesbury at the height of the Depression." If Wilson's three years at Oxford were comfortable in a conventional prewar, middle-class way, they also widened his social horizons, and laid the foundation for the kind of sympathy for ordinary people that emerges most clearly, for instance, in the "New Town" environment of *Late Call* (1964).

Angus Wilson left Oxford in the summer of 1935 with a respectable second-class degree in History. He had been thinking in terms of a post at the British Museum, and he obtained this in 1936, filling the interval with such things as secretarial work and helping his brother to run a restaurant.[18] He did not, however, find the job of cataloging and other routine library duties at all fulfilling, and though dissatisfaction was partly kept at bay by left-wing "busy political work to prevent the coming of war" (*WG,* 103), it must also have been deepened by the increasing uncertainties of the late 1930s: both the international ones and those familial ones experienced in his headmaster-brother's "melancholy, Chekhovian house" (*WG,* 97) near Seaford, where his relatives nervously awaited ultimate financial ruin. From 1936 until the outbreak of war, Wilson was alternately possessed by wishes to arrest time and to speed it toward the inevitable debâcle. In 1938, as the Germans marched into Czechoslovakia, Wilson's father, to whom he had been emotionally extremely close since his mother's death nine years before, died at the age of seventy-three. This event and the taut, mixed feelings surrounding it were reproduced some ten years later in Wilson's "A Story of Historical Interest."

The public and personal tensions which affected Wilson at the end of the 1930s were exacerbated by his experiences during World War II from 1941, not in the Armed Forces but in "a large inter-service organisation": a hush-hush operation, under the aegis of the Foreign Office, in "a somewhat dreary South Midlands countryside" (*WG,* 106). This was at Bletchley Park in Buckinghamshire, where intelligence work was brought to bear on cracking German machine codes. Wilson's colleagues there included "tough-minded dons in service uniform." This competitive environment was not to be mastered by Wilson's previously successful efforts to be friendly and to entertain, and though the people on whom he was billeted were kind, they were also culturally alien: a Methodist widow and her daughter who read and reread Bunyan's *Holy War* and found chain-smoking incomprehensible.

Since petrol was rationed Wilson was "marooned almost each night for almost four years" (*WG,* 19), and forced by his loneliness into an introspection quite new to one whose previous experience had been almost entirely social. His physical environment, a landscape whose pastoral was intersected by a Victorian canal and "under continuous threat of ugly urbanization," was quite different from the Sussex weald and downland in which he had spent congenial prewar weekends with friends and family, and it inspired in him an "almost suicidal melancholy" (*WG,* 106). In this atmosphere Wilson "fell really in love for the first time," but as a consequence only found himself confronting the recognition that he was a less pleasant person than he had thought, behaving demandingly and giving pain. His dreary wartime context, a hell of other people, is reflected in his story "Christmas Day in the Workhouse," and the jealous affection of Thea—aged just under thirty as he then was—for the upper-class Stephanie Reppington is perhaps a transposition of his strained emotional state.

"In all quarters, in love, with so-called inanimate nature, I found the impossibility of communication" (*WG,* 21). So Wilson summed up in *The Wild Garden* his psychological nadir, the nervous breakdown he suffered in 1944. But if isolation brought to a head pressures that had been building up for some years, it also, by forcing him to reflect on himself and his past life, led him "to rearrange my experience in imaginative terms, to try to make sense by making fictional patterns" (*WG,* 20). What life had lost, art had to rediscover. Advised by a psychotherapist to write as a form of occupational therapy, Wilson did not immediately do so. But when, in 1946, emerging from mental illness and back at the British Museum, he started to write as a way of "diversifying my time,"[19] it was not only in a mood of "feverish excitement" but with a force and authority that gained immediate recognition. The more powerfully for being so long unexamined, the conflicting emotions and patterns of Wilson's earlier life rose to the surface.

Since 1949

In *The Wild Garden* Angus Wilson says that he once felt he had become a writer by "pure accident." Later he did not think so, and he was surely right. From first story in 1946 to the first and highly successful collection in 1949 was too rapid a progress for that, and since then he has securely established himself as a novelist who has gone on developing the motifs and material implanted by his formative years while also being able to respond to the changes of the world about him.

Wilson remained a member of the British Museum staff, however, until 1955. The year of publication of *The Wrong Set,* 1949, was also the year in which he was appointed to a more congenial post there, that of Deputy Superintendent of the Reading Room. There, sitting on a raised dais in the center, he felt "very much like . . . a spider in its web," and observed "a vast variety of human types,"[20] some of whom, from cloakroom attendants to academics and administrators, found their way into his fiction.

In 1955 Wilson moved from London to a cottage near the village of Bradfield St. George in Suffolk, in "that undulating, yet hardly hilly country that I most love" (*WG,* 108), in order to concentrate full-time on his writing; though he also kept an apartment in the Dolphin Square block not far from Westminster School. In the country, slowly cultivating and bringing under control "a much neglected garden," he had returned in some degree to the pioneer childhood of his colonial mother, while still retaining ties with the London life he had led with both his parents in their later days. Since 1955 his chosen habits as a professional writer have combined mobility and rootedness; lecture visits abroad and twelve years as Visiting Professor of English Literature at the new University of East Anglia; critical study of the work of other novelists and the creation of his own. And in becoming one of the most notable practitioners of the novel in England since the war, Angus Wilson has also re-become, in a more memorable and public way, the entertainer with the desire to please that he was as a child and a young man before it.

Chapter Two

"Trifle Angus Wilson": Two Volumes of Short Stories

"Mr. Wilson is a satirist," roundly declared an anonymous reviewer when *The Wrong Set* appeared in 1949.[1] Since many of its stories, and many of those in *Such Darling Dodos* (1950), are lively, sharp, observant, and particularly concerned with social relationships and social class, it is not very surprising that they should have prompted a reviewer, pressed for time and space, to use this convenient label. "Satire" is also a term that Wilson himself employs quite frequently in *The Wild Garden* when discussing his early work.

At the same time, however, Wilson has denied any idea that satirizing people is the whole of his intention (*WG,* 27), and it is apparent that he attaches little theoretical weight to his use of the term *satire*. As he indicated to Michael Millgate in 1957, satire for him "implies an abstract philosophy that I don't have."[2] Though an acute commentator on human behavior, he is neither out to change it nor is he in general malicious about it. Wilson himself prefers to think of his work as "comedy of manners,"[3] and it would be a strange reader who rarely found anything to laugh at in the short stories; but they often mingle pathos with their comedy, sometimes provoking a nice mixture of distaste and sympathy in response to one and the same character or situation. And there are times when his chosen term "comedy of manners" cannot be accepted at all: stories like "Raspberry Jam," "Mummy to the Rescue," and "Necessity's Child" are not in the least funny.

Most of Wilson's short stories, which are largely a fictional expression of elements in his learning and working life up to the end of World War II, belong to the first few years of his life as a writer from 1946 onwards. He turned first to the short story for the simplest of practical reasons: as a full-time official of the British Museum he lacked the leisure for extended production. Short stories could be written in a weekend and even, as in the case of "Raspberry Jam," in a day. A sense of glibness and falsity is rarely, however, the impression these quickly written stories create. Rather, one has the feeling of an imaginative ferment, of material saved up for years and suddenly brought into focus.

In a review, published in 1954, of the work of other short-story writers Wilson indicated clearly the kind of short story, in a technical sense, that he himself had been trying to write. A keen admirer of Elizabeth Bowen,[4] he agreed with her contention that the short story, as a form, is nearer to the play and the poem than to the novel. Like the play, it needs to be compressed, and involves "climax, surprise and other directly artful methods of presentation"; like the poem, it uses "allusion, symbolism and overtone."[5] While admitting the influence of this view from the mid-1930s onwards, Wilson felt bound to point out that the situation in the first three decades of the century had been otherwise, the short story following the novel in changing from a storytelling medium into a vehicle for interior consciousness:

The classic short story of Mr. Maugham's era, with its emphasis on narrative and surprise, proved too tight to convey the flow of sensitivity which to Katherine Mansfield was the essence both of art and life. By injecting greater sublety of mood and deeper levels of consciousness, she almost succeeded in destroying the form and reducing short stories to "sketches."[6]

The efforts of short-story writers since 1939, Wilson said, had been directed to "trying to tie the two threads together"—the two threads being narrative form and significant emotional content. Thus, in effect, the view of the short story expressed by Elizabeth Bowen almost as an article of faith was in fact the hard-won result of a shift in literary taste, of which Wilson's short stories are a part. They mix, in varying proportions, the devices of drama and poetry, and attempt to combine the forward movement of story with the revelation of personality by means of thought processes.

The Wrong Set (1949)

Angus ·Wilson also spoke, in the review already referred to, of the need for a collection of short stories to hang together, to have some sort of unity. Of the collections he was reviewing, he singled out Louis Auchincloss's *The Romantic Egoists* as the best in this respect. Wilson, a liberal humanist, did not approve of Auchincloss's "arrogant, neo-aristocratic" outlook, but it had had a good effect artistically, producing a book of stories with "a strict social framework and

a convinced social standpoint." The coherence of Wilson's own earliest collections, both *The Wrong Set* and *Such Darling Dodos,* is equally
recognizable, though his middle-class framework is fluid rather than
strict, and his social standpoint, that of a convinced liberal with an
instinct for tolerance, allows for the inspection and questioning of
values rather than for their dogmatic presentation. A characteristic
conformation of Wilson's stories was pointed out by Kingsley Amis
in 1957: "his subject is most often the explosions and embarrass-
ments touched off when people of different class, training or culture
are made to confront one another."[7] There is also in his work a clash
of generations: on the personal level, between child and adult; on the
public level, brought about by the social and political changes that
gradually took place as the middle-class world in which Wilson grew
up emotionally was displaced by the postwar triumph—as it then
seemed—of the left-wing ideas he had espoused intellectually.

The unity of Wilson's short stories lies essentially in their atmosphere and their milieu, which are characterized by personal uncertainty, social precariousness, and an emotional ambivalence that
allows incidents and persons to be funny and pathetic at the same
time. A further cognate element in them, commented on by Wilson
himself in 1963, is a "pervasive raffishness,"[8] the source of which was
his own experience of "reduced" gentlewoman in Kensington hotels
and "old school tie" men down on their luck. (One of Wilson's
brothers had had to sell vacuum cleaners door to door after World
War I.) Before examining some of the stories for their individual
qualities, it is instructive to see how their group identity was perceived and rendered, in telling caricature, by one ordinary reader at
the time. In the early 1950s the *New Statesman,* which regularly ran
a humorous literary competition feature, asked readers to submit
cooking recipes that caught the manner of an important writer. The
fact that Angus Wilson, so soon after he had started to publish, was
one of the set topics, indicates by itself the impact he had made. June
F. Mercer's punning recipe for "Trifle Angus Wilson" brilliantly
combines some of the ingredients of his fictional world and the way
he was seen as presenting it:

Take your prettiest dish (never mind if it has a few tiny cracks), and line it
with alternate layers of crystallised pansies and light flaky spongers. Souse
the whole liberally with wine. Now place one dehydrated man (or slightly
less), in a narrow container and smother with one middle-class mother
steeped in saccharine and water. Choose a good-sized mother, with the flesh

firm, or only slightly flaccid. For extra flavour add a precarious social position. Leave the mixture to curdle. This will not take long, and it may then be added to the dish. Skim the top off a pint of wit, stiffen with restrained moral fervour, and whip up into whorls on top of the trifle. Decorate with light highbrow touches.

N.B. The secret of preparing the trifle is for the ingredients to get heated, while the cook remains perfectly cool. This will ensure exactly the wrong set.[9]

"Saturnalia," set at a staff-and-residents' dance in a small hotel in South Kensington on New Year's Eve, 1931, indicates the loosening effects of drink on the prewar class structure. The social spectrum ranges from a retired Colonial governor who quotes Greek and unsuccessfully pursues a good-looking page, down to Gloria, the pretty waitress who gets fondled by Bruce Talfourd-Rich, and Tom, the handsome Irish porter who almost succeeds in "making" Bruce's "injured wife," Claire, a woman tempted by thoughts of Lady Chatterley's lover while trying to maintain "a Knightsbridge exterior with a Kensington purse." The precarious pivot of this not-very-merry social roundabout is Stella Hennessy, who has "buckled to" after the economic crash and manages the hotel in order to maintain her son at public school. The cost to her of her sacrifice and "drudgery," in terms of internal coarsening, is economically suggested by the contrast between the "dove grey tulle" she wears and the hardness of her eyes, like "boot buttons," when she snubs Tom's blarneying advances: her new position, on the edge of gentility, seems too close to his for comfort. The claustrophobia and increasing heat of the evening are well conveyed by the dense look on the page of its long paragraphs, packed with snatches of dialogue and fleeting thoughts—a technique that Wilson also employs in "Crazy Crowd" to express Peter's sexual tension, trapped among the uncongenial Cockshutts. In both stories, as in several others, there is explosive release of the built-up tension in verbal violence which gives an almost orgasmic pleasure to the reader: in "Crazy Crowd" Peter attacks his lover Jenny's self-satisfied approval of the "crazy" quality of her family by rejecting it as repellent, so furiously that she can only silence him by pulling him on top of her in a direct sexual advance. In "Saturnalia" Gloria rejects the high moral tone taken by Stella who, jealous of Gloria's greater success with Bruce, takes the opportunity of her drunkenness to dismiss her from the hotel: "You silly old cow . . .

you won't send me away, you won't, not on your ruddy life. I know too much about you, my treasure, old Mother have me if you like Hennessy." At the end of "Saturnalia" a measure of order is restored when Claire dances with her husband, but the frustrations and antipathies of the crumbling social system have emerged unmistakably.

Wilson wrote "Saturnalia" in 1947, but set it in 1931 partly in order to exploit an ironic contrast[10] between the past, when the middle classes and their protective social distinctions still had some meaning, and the present, in which they were becoming obsolete. The title story, "The Wrong Set," is placed in the gray postwar Socialist world of clothing coupons and restricted foreign travel, in which earnest young students like Norman Hackett take part in Communist demonstrations and the faded remains of the old guard, represented by the moustached and monocled sponger, Major Trevor Cawston, eke out their existence between bed-sitting rooms in Earl's Court and sleazy Soho nightclubs in which they can tell snide stories about Prime Minister Attlee.

Though not hostile to either Norman or the disreputable Major, who at least know which social "set" they belong to, Wilson reserves most of his sympathy for the confused and good-hearted Vi, the pianist at the Passion Fruit Club, who is Norman's aunt and Trevor's mistress (and provider). Vi really belongs to neither set: to her working-class relatives she appears disreputable because she is not married to Trevor, while she aspires to the propriety of "wife" and clings to outmoded middle-class notions that "class told." Vi is in fact a social victim, expendable; but even when she loses her job—just after she has treated the club's Italian-cockney owner to a drink—she cannot perceive this. There is obvious irony in her telegraphed message to her sister that Norman is "in the Wrong Set," but she does not send it "to get some of her own back,"[11] as Jay. L. Halio, with uncharacteristic imperceptiveness, has written. Set adrift by the loss of her job, she may be seen as hanging on to a sense of her own identity by asserting her responsible role as aunt; she herself, in a semi-drunken mood of desperation that is both comical and moving, sees it as her "duty" as a "Conservative" to try to keep Norman out of "the hands of the Reds," and her final "Mayfair" attempts at dignity are impressive as well as pathetic.

"The Wrong Set" is a triumph of compression: its span of action covers only twenty-four hours, but its use of significant, sharply observed detail—not only at Vi's club but in Earl's Court and at Norman's lodgings in northwest London—enables Wilson to create in the space of ten pages a microcosm of changing British society. Even briefer, but also less comprehensive, is "Realpolitik," which reveals in its title and its neat, dramatic form the cold winds blowing through the postwar world. John Hobday, a newly appointed art gallery curator, confronts with careerist efficiency the old department heads who despise his manner and methods. "Hardboiled" as these scholarly idealists are, their poor committee methods are no match for Hobday's ruthless incisiveness, a quality made worse by the false geniality that accompanies it.

A more moving clash of opposites occurs in the triangular situation of "Fresh Air Fiend." Here again, as with "'The Wrong Set" and "Realpolitik," a cliché of speech is taken as a title and given an ironic dimension in the story that follows. It is Elspeth Eccles, former pupil and now research assistant of Professor Searle, who wishes to open windows and let in some air; but though, unlike John Hobday, she does not inspire simple dislike, the unexpected result of her action, announced by a similar twist at the end, proves how disastrous, indeed how counterproductive, can be the attempts of the younger generation to cut through the protective facades maintained by their elders.

Professor Searle is perhaps the first example in Wilson's work of the liberal whose decent principles and instincts do not enable him to cope with family problems: Bernard Sands of *Hemlock and After* and Gerald Middleton of *Anglo-Saxon Attitudes* are more fully drawn versions of the type. Wilson's sympathy for him is conveyed partly in a private code—part of his research, shared with Elspeth, is on Shelley, who was "a much-loved hero figure" in Wilson's own "mythology" (*WG*, 130)—but it is also evident in the guilt feelings that Searle expresses about his wife, Miranda, whose secret drinking is a consequence of her son's death and of the uncongenial life she has had to lead as the wife of an Oxford don. For Elspeth, the important problem is Searle's work, which he should be free to concentrate on: she hero-worships her professor and cannot bear to think of him as chained to the wreck of a former society beauty.

The tensions between Elspeth and Miranda, beautifully caught in their barbed, mutually patronizing exchanges in the garden, come to a head in the evening after dinner. Utterly drunk, Miranda interrupts her husband's tête-à-tête with Elspeth, making unworthy insinuations and accusing him of being "no great cop" in bed. The provocation results in Elspeth's slapping her face, Miranda's collapsing in tears, and, as is ironically revealed at the end, in Searle's subsequent nervous breakdown. The cause of this, we are left to infer, is not simply his own embarrassment, but distress that his wife's state should have been witnessed by a third party. His feelings had not "become hardened to the routine."

One is sorry for Searle; but Wilson's most instinctive sympathies seem to lie with Miranda, whose thwarted appetite for life has been channeled into gardening, and whose outrageous shocking of the "wretched middle-class norm" of other dons' wives he reports with relish. In Elspeth's attempts to draw her out—to get her, as Miranda scornfully puts it, to "share"—there is rather too much of the condescension of a social worker. Certainly her retort to Elspeth's new-fangled psychoanalytic jargon about a "well-adjusted view of life" carries a merited old-world sting: " 'Adjusted' never connects with 'life' for me, only with 'shoulder strap.' "

The *Times Literary Supplement* review of *The Wrong Set* noted "passages strongly reminiscent of Virginia Woolf,"[12] and there is much truth in the observation. Wilson read a great deal of her work in adolescence, and though he said in 1957 that he was "in great reaction against" her,[13] he also admitted that such reading could go very deep. His recurrent use of interior monologues, short or long, of the third-person and, less commonly, the first-person variety, indicates that it did. The first paragraph of "Fresh Air Fiend"—the first thing that a reader of Angus Wilson in 1947 would have encountered—is a good example, particularly in view of its telling use of the Woolfian pronoun "one." Miranda Searle, explicitly linked with Bloomsbury by being compared to Lady Ottoline Morrell, is discovered musing among her flowers: Woolfian style is used to describe a characteristic posture of the Virginia Woolf heroine.

Virginia Woolf's influence can also be felt in the long third-person interior monologues of Laura and Flo in the South African story "Union Reunion." In this story influence shades into literary parody in the first-person monologue of Minnie, which makes use of the "simple sentence" technique of *The Waves* in order to present a character who would be more at home in the pages of a Harlequin Romance:

"If the Kaffirs attacked 'The Maples' " thought Minnie, "I should have no man to defend me. Flo has Stanley and Laura has Harry, and Edie has her boys. I have no man. No woman was made to be petted and cared for more than me and yet I have no one. My hair is a lovely corn colour and my figure is beautiful . . . I trace figures in the sand with the tip of my cream lace parasol, but I do not look up. I am playing with him as Woman must."[14]

Another example of Wilson's tendency to mimic, perhaps unconsciously, a writer against whom he is in conscious reaction, occurs in "Significant Experience," set in the South of France which Wilson himself had visited a number of times in the 1930s. This time the writer is Aldous Huxley, whose early heroes the "aesthetic" Jeremy somewhat resembles—though in his "very English intellectual, very Pirates of Penzance" clothes he is also a product of a strong "camp" vein in Wilson himself. Jeremy's aspirations, as he tries to disentangle himself from Prue, the sensual "older woman" with whom he has had an affaire, have distinct overtones of the "sophisticated" novels that Aldous Huxley published in the 1920s and that Wilson read as a Westminster schoolboy:

His thoughts leapt forward all the time to his future, to his freedom—he would visit Aigues Mortes and Montpellier, wander up through Arles and Nimes, perhaps see the Burgundian tombs at Auxerre, he would read the new Montherlant he had bought in Paris, he might even write some poems again. (*WS*, 174)

The interior monologue method associated with Virginia Woolf is used in one of Wilson's most directly personal stories, "A Story of Historical Interest," which he has described as "an almost direct relation of my father's death in which I have cast myself in the role of a daughter" (*WG*, 48–49). Interior monologue is, however, used in a regular pattern of alternation with narrative. The method has affinities with that of "Mother's Sense of Fun," its thematic mirror-image: this consists of two large blocks, separated by some weeks, each of which proceeds internally by means of flashback; the story concluding, in the present, with a substantial shift of emotional perspective. But "A Story of Historical Interest" is longer and more complex, its sequence of internal flashbacks digging deeply into the personality of Lois Gorringe and her last days with her paralyzed father in a Kensington hotel, while she sits beside him in the ambulance on its bumpy way to her brother's house in Tunbridge Wells and the children's home in which he finally dies. The gradual deathward movement of Lois's father is paralleled in the public world by Neville Chamberlain's delaying tactics to prevent war—a fact which gives an

ironic ring to the title, though of course this also refers to the story's
biographical aspect.

The flashbacks progressively reveal Lois's devoted but inexpert efforts to look after her father, her genteel distaste for the vulgar, sexy
Irish nurse who can do it better, her unsuccessful interview with the
hotel manageress, whose refusal to let Mr. Gorringe stay in the hotel
threatens to end his daughter's monopoly of devotion, and her discussion with Dr. Filby, who wants to move him to a hospital. Lois
genuinely loves her father, but her horror at the last possibility leads
her to thoughts, however brief, of such hysterical absurdity that one
wonders whether their closeness is good for her: "They would take
him away from her, put him with the incurables. No! O God ! no,
rather let him die than that, she said half aloud" (WS, 80). Inside
Lois's selflessness there is a dangerous sentimental streak. She needs
her father at least as much as he needs her, and her reluctance to let
even her married brother Harold take care of him reinforces one's
sense of her dependence on a pattern that has lasted since her
mother's death.

Forced, by the chain of circumstances revealed in the flashbacks, to
yield to the inevitable, Lois finally arrives with her father at Harold's
house. There, though we see the cheerful vulgarity of Harold and
Daisy through Lois's "superior" eyes, their matter-of-fact shouldering
of the family "burden" reveals the strained, theatrical quality that accompanies Lois's more sensitive attitudes. And when they all visit
Mr. Gorringe at the curious nursing home for unwanted children in
which Harold's combination of meanness and good sense has placed
him, even Lois notices his new perkiness and recognizes the fact that
he does "not seem to mind" the businesslike, babying way he is
treated.

It may be that, away from the hothouse of Lois's devotion, Mr.
Gorringe is free to become again the "raffish old sport"[15] he used to
be: perhaps, as with the nurse, Lois has made the mistake of seeing
depths in him "where they don't exist." Or perhaps he is just declin-
ing into second childhood. Whichever it is, Lois's distress is evident
in her quick departure. She promises to come and see him again, but
when in the last section she learns he has gone into a terminal coma,
she fails to do so, saying to a puzzled Daisy: "It's really only of historical interest." Without meaning to, she has repeated the phrase
Dr. Filby used when he suggested that her father might have tertiary
syphilis—something which, at this stage, cannot make his death any

more likely than it already is. The medical detail is merely an irrelevant historical fact, like Lois's long-cherished relationship with a father who is unlikely to regain consciousness and ask for her by name.

Her final action, going out to meet "hundreds of interesting, new people," has a touch of desperation in it that counteracts the appearance of callousness. The action contains both an element of resentment and an element of belated, healthy self-assertion; but it also proceeds from the need to turn away from a past now irrevocably lost. That regret is hidden beneath Lois's brisk behavior can perhaps be inferred from the opposite ending of "Mother's Sense of Fun," where Donald Carrington's detestation of his mother while she is alive unexpectedly changes to a horrible sense of loneliness when she is dead.

Emotional ambivalence, related to the need Angus Wilson himself felt to emerge from the protective yet stifling companionships of his early life, gives many of his stories what he has called "the fierceness that is their strength" (*WG*, 28). Many of them are concerned with a quality he refers to as "preserved innocence" (*WG*, 28)—an innocence (or ignorance) properly associated with childhood, but becoming harmful when retained in adult life. The self-satisfied insularity of the Cockshutt family in "Crazy Crowd" is a satirical example of it, the "uneducated" class-loyalties of Vi in "The Wrong Set" a more touching one. But the quality is most powerfully investigated in Wilson's first story, "Raspberry Jam," and with a fierceness that shocked early reviewers, one of them calling its conclusion—the torturing of a bullfinch by two drunken old ladies—"blood-curdling,"[16] another seeing it as an illustration of Wilson's "taste for brutality."[17]

The ending of "Raspberry Jam" is indeed unpleasant, the more so because it involves the momentary, horrified complicity of Johnnie, the boy on the verge of puberty who witnesses it; Johnnie, Wilson has said, is "drawn directly from myself as I had been at that age" (*WG*, 25), and Wilson had admitted being "barbarously cruel to insects," and burning moths in a candle flame at fifteen (*WG*, 80). But such sadistic impulses, however deplorable, are hardly rare; what is more important—indeed the moral point of the story—is the incident's shock-value for Johnnie, in terminating abruptly his friendship with the two old ladies, whose congeniality as companions in imagination is now seen to be rooted in a failure to grow up, an inability to cope with an uncongenial adult world.

Both the structure and the narrative method of "Raspberry Jam" are extremely ingenious. The emotional force of the tale derives from

its sticking for much of the time to Johnnie's own view of events and
the three worlds in which he lives: his anthropomorphic, book-influ-
enced games with his toy animals; his "love-starved" homelife among
"unimaginative adults" who on the one hand urge him to grow up
into their duller world and, on the other, like pompous, romantic
Mr. Codrington, advocate retaining "the fantasies, the imaginative
games of childhood, even at the expense of a little fear" (WS, 145);
his friendship with the two colorful, upper-class old ladies, Marian
and Dolly Swindale, who "were the first people he had met who liked
what he liked and as he liked it" (WS, 150). One is led to sympathize
with Johnnie in his loneliness, his reluctance to grow up ("one always
seemed to be getting too old for something"; WS, 147) and his delight in the company of the two sisters, who share his imaginative
games, enlarge his horizons by their recollections, and value the
"odd" and the "fantastic." Interwoven with Johnnie's impressions,
however, and with his intense protectiveness toward the old ladies,
whom their Sussex village neighbors think "old and useless and in the
way," are recurrent suggestions from Wilson's authorial voice that
their engaging dottiness is not far from insanity, that their kindness
to Johnnie is a form of mental retardation, and that their enlisting of
his protective instincts proceeds from persecution mania. (They have,
in fact, previously been "put away.") Yet the authorial voice, though
judicial, is also compassionate, revealing the sisters—the gruff, sol-
dierly Marian, the painted, "naughty" Dolly, who makes eyes at bus
conductors—as pathetic survivals of a former age: they outrage their
neighbors, but can also be seen as misunderstood and rejected by
them.

Wilson's structuring of the story, which inverts its time sequence,
also creates a complex emotional reaction in the reader. From Johnnie's point of view, the terrible climax has already taken place; from
the reader's, it has still to come. Thus Johnnie is perceived adjusting
to life without his friends, and to his new vision of them as dangerous, before the reader knows why. Johnnie's memories of his pleasure
in their company serve the double purpose of creating suspense and
enlisting sympathy, a sympathy both widened and edged with tension as the week leading up to the fateful Thursday is described in
terms of the sisters' experience: their village quarrels, their uncharacteristic mutual falling-out, and the separate drinking bouts that
follow it. When, therefore, Wilson's elaborate flashback reaches
Johnnie's visit, the torturing of their bullfinch "prisoner" is both un-

derstandable from their crazed point of view (to them it is a thief of the raspberries they had intended for their beloved guest and a captured "spy" from the hostile village), and horrifying from Johnnie's.

The relation of climax and flashback carries the reader in an ever-renewed circle from the "end" of the story to the beginning. Johnnie's attempt to expunge the incident from his mind by stamping the dead bullfinch into "a lump of raspberry jam"[18] on the farmhouse floor explains his nightmares (reported by his mother soon after the story opens) and his screams when she offers him raspberry jam for tea. And his realization, in such a violent way, of the sisters' essential madness makes understandable his leaving the room when Mr. Codrington concludes his well-meaning eulogy of them by referring to "the imaginative games of childhood," as the "true magnificence of the Springtime of life." For Johnnie, the innocence of childhood has exacted too high a price.

"Preserved innocence" is not always so sympathetic as Johnnie's rococo fantasy-world with his animals, or even as the Swindale sisters' inability to move beyond memories of their Victorian father, the General. In some cases it can become what Wilson calls "a calculated refusal of imaginative compassion," as in "A Visit in Bad Taste," which he thinks of as his best story (*WG,* 42). It is also his shortest, and in it the touch of poetic symbolism of "Raspberry Jam" is replaced by a quasi-dramatic approach: the story is like a one-scene play, covering hardly more than an hour, in which speeches are counterpointed, with unobtrusive cunning, against actions that reveal their hollowness.

Margaret and Malcolm Tarrant, two apparent liberals who have built up in their carefully furnished home a place of "taste, . . . tolerance, . . . ease of living, . . . lack of dogmatism," are faced with the presence of Margaret's brother Arthur, a former bank manager and ex-public-school man who has, at sixty, just finished a prison term for "offences against children." With his air of "military precision" and his "overpressed" suit, Arthur belongs to the type of "old sport" represented by Mr. Gorringe and Major Cawston; but though his unease with his chilly relatives reveals him in a momentarily sympathetic light, Wilson chooses to play him down as a person in order to emphasize the lack of ordinary charity in Margaret's and Malcolm's response to him as a case.

Malcolm's "Covenanting ancestry" makes it impossible for him to forgive Arthur's crime, though on his own he might treat Arthur

himself kindly. The more decisive hostility to Arthur comes from
Margaret, whose unwillingness to have him in the house proceeds
from a kind of aesthetic snobbery: Arthur's manner is "servile," his
style of speech displeases her, she cannot stand his right-wing prejudices about her servants—while herself loathing the kind of working-
class people with whom his offenses have involved him. At Arthur's
trial Margaret enjoyed a "Dostoevskeyan mood" of high-flown literary
suffering; but now that Arthur is physically present again she wants
no more of him and even suggests—in a dramatic manner now reminiscent of Hedda Gabler's exhortations to Eilert Lövborg to "do it
beautifully"—that he may find suicide the best way out. Her liberalism is nothing more than a set of self-flattering gestures, a suite of
mental furniture that Arthur does not "go with."

    Her rejection of Arthur on grounds such as these comes over as
cold and despicable. Malcolm's attitude, at least intellectually, seems
to merit some respect. But the story's last phrase—"He remained
vaguely uneasy the whole evening" (WS, 139)—conveys, along with
its tautological pointer to the reader, the implication that Malcolm,
who feels culturally superior to his wife and thus should behave better, is at least equally to blame: his qualms will be forgotten so very
quickly. His underlying unity with Margaret, despite his not-iden-
tical opinions, is suggested by Wilson's use of telling movements, as
of actors on a stage. Just as Margaret, while talking, "rustled and
shimmered across the room to place a log on the great open fire" and
"speared a crystallised orange from its wooden box," so Malcolm "replaced his glass of port on the little table by his side" and "moved
his cigar dexterously so that the long grey ash fell into the ashtray
rather than onto his suit" (WS, 131–33). For all their liberal "lack of
dogmatism," they share an instinctive taste for gracious living which
the presence of Arthur, awkward and vulgar, can only spoil. More
bleakly than most of Wilson's stories, "A Visit in Bad Taste" has "a
kind of immediate ethical text,"[19] and its clarity is much aided by
the use of such silent gestures.

    "Et Dona Ferentes," written a month after "Raspberry Jam" (WG,
83), and printed at the end of the collection, is perhaps the richest
story in The Wrong Set. It combines all the aspects of Wilson's
method as a short-story writer, revealing its six characters through
the barbed exchanges of dramatic dialogue as well as through detailed
interior monologues, and moving the five-section narrative forward
against an unusual background for early Wilson, that of external na-

ture. It also suggests the interpersonal tensions of the basic situation—Monica Newman's jealousy and embarrassment at her husband's interest in a Swedish boy—by means of a brewing storm which bursts in lightning and subsides in rain. The story, presenting three generations of an English middle-class family and the disruptive stranger in their midst, anticipates the larger canvases of Wilson's novels.

The story's title, a reference to the famous line in Virgil's *Aeneid*, "Timeo Danaos et dona ferentes" (I fear the Greeks, especially when they bring gifts), encapsulates Monica Newman's viewpoint: the pendant that she rejects at the end is bought for her by her homosexually inclined husband, Edwin, at the malicious instigation of their teenage Swedish visitor, Sven Sodeblom, to whom he has taken a fancy and with whom he has disappeared from the family picnic. It is the possibility that Edwin will, through Sven's presence, succumb to powerful past temptations that partly explains Monica's edginess at the beginning of the story and entirely explains her waspishness toward Sven, whom she despises for his materialism and vanity, but also fears for his physical attractiveness and animal charm. Her edginess, however, is accompanied by guilt: in recently cutting down sex with Edwin, who is depicted as extremely youthful, she "had withdrawn her sympathy at the very moment Edwin needed it most," and feels that if anything happens she will be to blame. Edwin's disappearance from the picnic is followed by the bursting of the storm, whose flashes of lightning both cause and mimic Monica's rising hysteria.

Despite her love for Edwin, and her guilt feelings, which win the reader's sympathy, Monica's inability to relax outdoors, and her view of nature as "patterns of shape and colour" to be completed and improved by man, together with her basic lack of interest in sex, make it understandable that Edwin should feel stifled in her company. A lack of direct confrontation with life is also perceived by Edwin—and by the reader—in his daughter Elizabeth, who is going through a "priggish" religious phase, and in her bookish son Richard, whose sensitive involvement with Dostoevsky's *The Possessed* cannot yet translate itself into easy or tactful communication with real people. Mrs. Rackham, Edwin's mother-in-law, comes over as pleasant enough, in her detached way, and at the end gives useful practical help to enable Edwin and Monica to patch up their marriage at their London flat; but she is also presented as someone who, (unlike "one of those Virginia Woolf mothers") cannot fathom the emotions of others and indeed prefers to plunge into "her twenty-third reading of *Emma*"—a book that Wilson, generally an admirer of Jane Austen, sees as recommending self-satisfied insularity.[20]

Edwin's attempt to communicate with Sven does not, in the event, work out. What starts as a genuine wish to make amends to Sven for Monica's and his children's inhospitality by showing him some Saxon remains, develops into a wish to "get to know" him better by means of an overnight stay in a nearby town. Edwin's romantic attraction to Sven is seen both as a sympathetic wish to "break out" and renew his youth, and as slightly ridiculous. His hinting advances are too easily "placed" by Sven's sexual sophistication, which sees in them only the opportunity to acquire a present and to get his own back for Monica's "bitchiness" by alarming her. As it happens, Sven is a rampant heterosexual, and in turning out the contents of his shallow mind Wilson shows him as incapable of much emotion beyond a repellent narcissism: thinking of his earlier female conquests Sven sees himself as "so handsome he felt that sometimes he almost wanted himself."

The wry conclusion of this skillful, involving story—a story reminiscent of E. M. Forster in its picture of various "undeveloped hearts" and even more in its sense of landscape as a challenging force and its portrayal of the disturbing Sven as like Pan—shows Edwin reunited with Monica after his sudden return from Milkford bearing placatory gifts. Whether Sven's sexual unwillingness, or Edwin's thinking better of his wild impulse, has aborted the intended night in a hotel we are not told. In a sense, Edwin is well out of it: someone like Sven will find greener pastures back home, and Monica's feelings are still important to her husband. Nevertheless, the mixture of relief and regret in the final paragraph conveys the cost to Edwin of his return to the orthodoxy of the family fold:

Safe, thought Edwin, safe, thank God! But the room seemed without air, almost stifling. He threw open one of the windows and let in a refreshing breeze that blew across from the hills. (*WS*, 223)

Such Darling Dodos

After this fairly detailed treatment of *The Wrong Set*, it is not necessary to spend quite so much time on Wilson's second collection. The feelings, recollections, and social ambience out of which both volumes spring are to a large extent the same, though the stories in *Such Darling Dodos* sometimes have a certain emotional thinness (as in

"Sister Superior") and an element of exaggeration and contrivance (as in "A Little Companion") that suggest an imagination working at reduced pressure while the conscious mind makes a story out of an interesting idea.

"Rex Imperator," which derives its claustrophobic emotional atmosphere from the many vacations Wilson spent in the 1930s at his elder brother's house at Seaford, is a fictional version of that brother's relationship to the rest of the Wilson family: martyred by his relatives' parasitic dependence on him, Rex Palmer is also their "King Emperor" by virtue of having money for their support at his disposal. Offering a sharp study of the perverse operations of "Bourgeoisie Oblige," the story finely balances dislike of Rex's domineering ways and of the ingratitude they provoke in his relatives, with pained admiration for Rex's self-torturing sense of duty and a degree of sympathy for the pretensions by means of which his relatives cling to their human dignity: old Mr. Nicholson, Rex's garrulous father-in-law, is based on Wilson's own father, the archetypal "raffish old sport."

"Necessity's Child," like "Raspberry Jam," goes further back in Wilson's life, being a "near autobiography . . . of my last childhood years" at Bexhill. Rodney, unable to swim and poor at games, is presented as both unpleasantly sly and much to be pitied: excluded by his parents' closeness from the love he needs, he makes up stories in which he cuts a good figure and tells lies in order to gain notice and sympathy. His pathetic lies about his dependent invalid mother, which he tells to a friendly old couple encountered on the seafront, and the near-criminal lies that he later tells his aunt about them, both win him the same tribute: "I shall always think of you as a very brave boy." But the story ends with a nightmare vision of isolation no less powerful for deriving from Rodney's reading of *Moby Dick* and stories of the *Titanic* disaster. The story's final version of Rodney's ambivalent dependence on his "vanished" parents, as he struggles on a raft "with the ropes too securely tied" is given a more horrible, if melodramatic, twist at the end of "Mummy to the Rescue," in which the retarded Celia, having tied herself to the bed with the blue cardigan she associates with her drowned mother, chokes to death while dreaming that her mother is strangling her.

The attractive story "What Do Hippos Eat," which is printed last in the volume, has affinities with "The Wrong Set," though it is placed in the 1930s: Maurice Legge's better days as an ex-officer, embroidered by sentimental memory, seem to be well in the past. Like Trevor Cawston, he is now down on his luck in a boardinghouse in Earl's Court, but ever hopeful that something will turn up. In fact, something has: his landlady and mistress, Greta, twenty years younger than himself, who has risen from working-class origins but finds in Maurice a gentleman in whose company she can further polish her manners and feel a lady: "she was ready to forgive him anything as she watched him finger the knot of his old school tie whilst he studied the menu, and heard him refer to her as 'madam' when he finally gave the order." In being genuinely fond of the man she supports, Greta resembles Vi; but she is tougher-minded, not to be sponged on more than she wishes and not averse to putting Maurice in his financial place. The intricate interplay in their relationship of affection, self-interest, and class snobbery is shown in the course of a visit to the zoo, which brings out in both of them a vulgar, patronizing attitude to the animals, behavior of which Wilson disapproves (WG, 85–86), but which also probes the uneasiness and hostility that lurk beneath his showing-off and her "dopey jokes."

In the zoo, a series of incidents reveals Greta's money-emboldened vulgarity and Maurice's poverty-undermined snobbishness, both of which taint their genuine affection. These incidents culminate in Maurice's mad impulse to push Greta into the hippo pool. He is only restrained by the realization that to fail in his grand gesture of feeding Greta to the hippos, and thus set her completely against him, would be worse than to succeed. Ironically, the "childlike" Greta interprets his hands on her waist as a "touching" gesture, a public show of affection such as Maurice has taught her is "just not done." The misunderstanding turns potential melodrama into near-farce; but the incident crystallizes very successfully the tensions inherent in a changing society where those on the way down attempt communication with those on the way up.

A new element enters *Such Darling Dodos* in the title story. As well as being concerned to show, in his short stories, what he has called the "false standards" of the genteel or "new poor" middle classes— the type he knew from the Kensington hotels of his youth—Wilson also felt dissatisfaction with the "insufficient standards" (WG, 28–29) of the kind of middle-class liberals, or Fabian socialists, whom he had known as an undergraduate at Oxford and during his prewar years at the British Museum.

The precise cause of his disenchantment is not clear: "Such Darling Dodos," with its dense accumulation of small cultural details—the "oatmeal fabrics and unpolished oak" of "Courtwood," the puffed wheat and strong Indian tea which Tony is offered for breakfast, and the "sensible" clothes of his relatives, Priscilla and Robin, suggests that it may have been a distaste for the Fabians' personal style as much as any sense that their policies had failed. Wilson did not, in fact, turn away from a concern for social justice: in *The Wild Garden* he makes it clear that "the left-wing causes of Priscilla and Robin," for all their unfashionableness to the young, still seemed to him no less "worth-while in themselves" (*WG,* 29), and after he settled in Suffolk in 1955 he earned a local reputation as a "radical" by canvassing for the Labour Party.[21] One is left to infer in Wilson's postwar questioning of the way of life he had once espoused some sense that the whole pattern of prewar life had let him down—both his close involvement with his own Imperialist family and his friendships with substitute families in whose Socialism he had perhaps hoped to find a personal as well as a political panacea.

One hint Wilson does give of the reason for his dissatisfaction with a "progressive" life devoted to good causes, saying in *The Wild Garden* that "Robin and Priscilla lack . . . some poetry to illuminate them" (*WG,* 29). The lack is indicated, cattily, in Tony's reaction to the large, awkward Priscilla as she hovers by his bedroom door: "Surely . . . there must be some delinquent child or unmarried mother to claim her attention even at this hour of the morning." For Tony, an aesthete who grew up with his "ears full of Stravinsky and his eyes full of Bakst," it is pitiful that Priscilla can still "believe in this illusory paradise of refrigerators for all." Her type, worthy but gray, is immediately recognizable, and though Tony's opinions about her are undercut by our view of him in bed—a wrinkled pansy in a hair-net, wearing cold cream—an early authorial comment aims at our less equivocal assent, pointing to Priscilla's taste for human "pathos" and the committee and clinic work that expresses it as things that "fixed her emotionally as a child playing dolls' hospitals." Not only "poetry" but family piety takes second place to such a life of good works: Robin is dying, but he and Priscilla have decided this does not justify summoning their son Nick back from Germany, involved as he is in the important task of "reorganising the whole teaching syllabus at the Hochschule."

It is the approaching death of Robin, Socialist economics don but born a Catholic, that has brought Tony, with all the zeal of a Catholic convert, to his relatives' house in North Oxford. He has been prompted to come by an emotional letter from Priscilla in which she spoke of her fear of future loneliness. Tony, whose faith is vital to him but who has also, in the past, felt he has "missed the essentials of life" and envied his left-wing relatives' easy rapport with the politically minded young, has seen in Priscilla's uncharacteristic uncertainty a chance to demonstrate the superiority of his own values by convincing Robin and Priscilla of the greater importance of eternity and bringing Robin back to the faith. For Tony, their decision not to call their son home is a deep shock: with a sort of Catholic romanticism he has idealized their relationship as one that approaches "Christian marriage," and sees in this an achievement far greater than their good works and likely to outlast them.

Tony's visit does not succeed in its purpose, though in stating the case for faith and for "God's infinite mercy," he attains a real eloquence that transcends any self-interest in his motives. For Priscilla, and for Robin, it is what people achieve in life, for others, that matters, not how they face the "squalid" irrelevance of death: human works, not religious faith. Their side of the case, too, is put with an equivalent, if bleak, impressiveness, particularly by the cadaverous Robin: rereading William James's *The Varieties of Religious Experience* he has been able to find "nothing to accord with anything I had ever known."

In terms of its arguments, or rather its statements, "Such Darling Dodos" reaches an honest impasse: one is left uncertain which set of values is right; and choice between the two comes to depend on individual taste, style, or predisposition. The ironic conclusion of the story gives a kind of verbal victory to Tony; but it is an irony that cuts both ways. Michael and Harriet Eccleston, visiting "Courtwood" at the end, do not share the attitudes of Priscilla and Robin; they find something "theatrical" and inadequate in the "famous rally" to feed the Hunger Marchers from Jarrow, think the photographs of people "relaxing at Fabian summer schools" and carrying "incredible banners" something of a joke, prefer right-wing concepts of "responsibility" and order to left-wing notions of freedom, and feel some attraction toward religion. With such postwar new-style young people Tony at last feels at home, and in their company refers to Robin and Priscilla, with a slight touch of malice, as "dodos . . . but . . . such darling dodos." It is the last phrase of the story. Perhaps they are, and one feels some pity for their outmodedness. Just before the end, however, Tony has told the young people that "a good many of us thought quite differently" from Robin and Priscilla, and in Michael's reply there is a subtle indication that, all the same, Tony resembles them in one inescapable detail: " 'Oh naturally, Sir,' said Michael, he loved old world manners." Tony, too, is a dodo: the failures in communication, stemming from honestly held opinions, between members of the same generation are displaced, in the process of history, by the inevitable differences between one generation and the next.

The difficulty of escaping from the past, indeed from what seems almost the preordained shape of one's fate, is an important theme in "Totentanz," one of three stories that derive from Wilson's Bletchley years. (The other two are "Christmas Day in the Workhouse" and "Heart of Elm.") It also embodies on a grand scale the element of the supernatural that is peculiar to *Such Darling Dodos*, finding expression elsewhere in Celia's nightmare in "Mummy to the Rescue" and, more whimsically, in the mischievous alter-ego figure that haunts Miss Arkwright, the spinster of "A Little Companion." In its malevolent academic framework "Totentanz" has something in common with "Learning's Little Tribute," which depicts with minute, acidulous care the pretty hypocrisies and meanness of a group of academic hacks and pretentious litterateurs.

The origin of "Totentanz" lay in a visit Wilson made, for therapeutic purposes, after his nervous breakdown at Bletchley Park in 1944. He went to Scotland, to the small university town of St. Andrews; apart from Oxford, it was the only university town he had encountered. The place struck him as a very closed-in society, and one likely to be especially stifling to the wife of an academic there.[22] His eventual story, set in 1949, erects on this basic feeling—sympathy for a woman trapped in a constricting place—a construction that is very much larger than life, a kind of Northern Gothic fantasy in which initial exaggeration ("sub-arctic isolation . . . continual mists . . . perpetual north-east gales") gives place to inventions more and more bizarre and macabre, as if Wilson were writing out of his system the pressures of his nervous breakdown and his wartime sense of claustrophobia.

For Brian Capper, newly appointed to a Chair of Art History at London University, and his wife Isobel, who has simultaneously come into a legacy of half a million pounds, rescue from their stifling, provincial environment seems to have come only just in time. He is escaping from "the waters of Lethe" which are turning him from an academic "infant phenomenon" into a dull, pipe-wielding automaton, she from "the flames of hell," a burning consciousness of frustrated social ambition in a place unappreciative of her fashionable artistic taste. Neither of the Cappers is attractive, but Wilson's depiction of the smug mannerisms of local academic society makes it possible to sympathize with them in their stroke of luck, and in the summer weather of the university town even Brian's colleagues are able to forgive him for it, to "rejoice at a fellow-prisoner's release." At first, in London, both the Cappers find the smart kind of success they want, Brian's name carrying weight "at the High Tables of All Souls and King's," Isobel cultivating such (decidedly odd) luminaries as Professor Cadaver, the expert on ancient tombs; Lady Maude, the rich art-connoisseur; Guy Rice, the homosexual interior decorator and expert on chic taste in clothes and people; and Tanya Mule, the ravaged ex-beauty who knows all the illegal ways of managing well in austerity Britain.

If the names of Isobel's friends suggest, correctly, the influence on "Totentanz" of the black comedy of Evelyn Waugh, to whose *Decline and Fall* it bears a distinct resemblance, a short interlude passage set in Scotland brings in overtones of *Macbeth,* as the Master's wife and Miss Thurkill, described as "an evil bat" and "a barking jackal" respectively, express a sense of foreboding that (like the prophecies of the Weird Sisters) is difficult to distinguish from ill-wishing. And in fact the Cappers' new life soon goes awry: the bequest to Isobel, from her drowned aunt and uncle, contains a condition. The Cappers not only have to live in their benefactors' house, they must also live with two seven-foot-high statues of them, to be kept permanently in "that room in which they entertain their friends."

Having begun in a mode not too far from realism, "Totentanz" moves at this point into the world of grotesque fable—the "dead hand of the past" in white marble sculpture—and of sinister literary archetype: Macbeth and Lady Macbeth at the feast with Banquo's ghost visible for all to see. Guy Rice's clever suggestion that their first big reception be a *Totentanz*—a "Dance of Death" with the guests dressed in all variations of costume from Vampire and Corpse Eater to "the suicide of Chatterton"—seems the way to accommodate Isobel's ambitions as a hostess with the strange demand of her relatives. Unfortunately, Isobel's "greatest triumph" proves the end of her hopes, followed as it is by the actual suicide of Guy Rice, who is being blackmailed, the decapitation of Lady Maude by a burglar, and the death of Professor Cadaver as he tries to break open a grave in Brompton Cemetery—all of these events being described with ghou-

lish, operatic panache. Isobel declines into a state of apathetic com-
munion with "the two great monuments," hardly noticing that her
husband has turned into the hearty, hollow academic stereotype he
was threatening to become before he left his job in Scotland. There,
where it began, the story ends, with a malevolent exchange between
the Master's wife, a "huge, squat toad," and Miss Thurkill, a "writh-
ing . . . malicious snake." Having visited London in a vain attempt
to get a post herself, Miss Thurkill has noticed that the Capper house
is apparently shut up; the Master's wife replies "Got the
plague, I expect . . . took it from here."

In psychological terms this may well be the explanation: in the
Scottish university town "at least we know we're dead"; and the Cappers, in trying to escape something outside themselves, seem only to
have discovered it was inside all along. But Wilson's gross, blackly
comic inventiveness, worthy of Evelyn Waugh at his most destructive, turns this rueful insight into a fiction that exists brilliantly for
its own sake, and it is easy to understand why, in his *Spectator* review
of 1954, he should have said: "There is nothing more satisfactory, as
I know from experience, than writing a macabre or a morbid short
story."[23]

Wilson as a Short-Story Writer

Wilson's satisfaction with "Totentanz'— whose heartless yet zest-
ful extravagance gives it a unique place among his short stories—is
a feeling his readers have generally experienced toward his two earliest collections as a whole. They are a most distinguished contribution
to the genre, and display such versatility of technique and variation
of detail that no story seems merely to repeat another, even though
they proceed from a mental world recognizably Wilson's own and
thus characterized, like that of any writer, by recurrent patterns and
underlying assumptions. The world of Wilson's short stories assumes
a close emotional link (whether present or desired) between children
and parents, an "apprehension of moral ambiguity in relationships"
(*WG,* 98), a sense of the comedy and pathos of human life, and a
preference for the near-at-hand of the observer rather than for the remote distances of the visionary.

Lying behind all these aspects is the central reality of Wilson's
short stories: they present a world of people. Nature is not of much
importance in them, and the divine or the eternal even less. It is no-

ticeable that the people in Wilson's short stories are rarely alone; when they are, it is because their relationships are giving them trouble, not because they are seeking solitude. Through interior monologue Wilson is adept at presenting their inner worlds, but his even more striking gift is for the personal or social exchange of dialogue, which in his stories is revealingly specific and sharply credible to the ear. Similarly acute is Wilson's eye for the betraying detail of dress, decor, or behavior. Both his dialogue and his description present the seething, unregenerate vitality and the failings of human beings—not "types," as a reviewer of *Such Darling Dodos*[24] felt, but individuals— with an honesty that gave many of his original readers a sense of release. In Wilson's stories they recognized with delighted shock the little eccentricities, the irritating mannerisms of speech and attitude, that other writers had ignored or failed to spot. But Wilson's concern to balance failings with virtues, or at least to contrast the faults of one person with those of another, insures an overall atmosphere of tolerance and fairness: he is a writer who notices, unsparingly, but not one who despises. Only occasionally does his presentation of people fail to ring true, as when for instance, in "Learning's Little Tribute," he puts into the mouth of the chief encyclopedist Mr. Brunton a contextually incredible tirade against the decent Mrs. Craddock.

The majority of Wilson's stories reveal individual situations at some point of crisis or decision, the classic formula of the short story which concentrates on only a short period of time or a small group of people. Some, however, imply a possibility of expansion: "Union Reunion" and "Et Dona Ferentes," with their larger casts; "A Little Companion" and "Totentanz," with their longer time-scales; "Heart of Elm" with its mention of Constance Graham's ten-year past relationship with her faithful retainer Ellen. There is, also, in "Such Darling Dodos," the suggestion of material lying between past and present that could be explored at greater length. Though with his first two volumes Wilson demonstrates a remarkable mastery of the short story, his turning after 1950 to the larger and more complex form of the novel comes as no surprise.

Chapter Three
Distressed Liberals and Others

Angus Wilson's novels began to appear in the 1950s, a decade which also saw the emergence of the group of writers labeled by journalism "Angry Young Men": Kingsley Amis, John Wain, Alan Sillitoe, John Braine, John Osborne. Of lower-middle-class origin, these writers had grown up during World War II and had in common an impatience with the monopoly which still seemed to be exercised after it by upper-middle-class cultural attitudes and literary cliques. For them, the privileged liberal humanism represented by such Bloomsbury writers as E. M. Forster and Virginia Woolf was at best an irrelevance, at worst an obstruction. Since the early short stories of Angus Wilson exercised themselves in puncturing bourgeois affectations of superiority and in exposing the weakness of the liberal humanist outlook, he too was seen for a time as an agent of postwar change, a kind of "fresh-air fiend."

Every period tends to notice in the work of people who belong to it those elements that seem to partake of some perceived "spirit of the age," and Wilson was not altogether wrongly aligned, at the start of his career, with writers a decade or so younger than himself. Nevertheless, it is worth noticing that he was nearly forty when his first novel *Hemlock and After* appeared in 1952, and had not only grown up at a time when the influence of "Bloomsbury" was still very real, but belonged, however edgily, to the southern, metropolitan, upper-middle-class world to which Bloomsbury literature was mainly addressed, and in which its liberal humanist assumptions—agnosticism, openmindedness, tolerance, and respect for the individual—typically operated. If the hero of *Hemlock and After,* Bernard Sands, has a name that suggests insecurity and impermanence, he is nevertheless seen to have virtues; if he is held up for inspection rather than uncritical admiration, he is viewed with the sympathy of a writer who understands his milieu. Moreover, the postwar world into which Bernard and his wife Ella survive, like more warmly delineated versions of Robin and Priscilla Harker in "Such Darling Dodos," is not presented by Wilson as having a better system of values to replace theirs.

Indeed, despite their publication and usual location in the contemporary postwar world, Wilson's novels derive many of their values, and much of their vitality, from the prewar one. It does not seem accidental that, whereas the heroes of the earliest work of Amis, Wain, Sillitoe, Braine, and Osborne are the same age as, or younger than, their authors, Wilson's first hero is nearly twenty years older. Much of the interest of Wilson's contribution to the literature of the 1950s lies precisely in his viewpoint as a writer almost in middle age when the decade opened, and thus capable of a perspective on it socially and culturally different from that of the writers who, by a historical accident, were his publishing contemporaries. Twenty years later, speaking of *Hemlock and After* in 1971, Wilson made quite clear the importance he attached to liberal humanism, despite his presentation in 1952 of its limitations: "It seems to me that what is left of liberal humanism is one of the most hopeful forces in the world . . . even if its prestige is no longer so great as it once was."[1]

Hemlock and After (1952)

Angus Wilson's first, and shortest, novel was written in 1951 during a leave of four weeks from his post as Deputy Superintendent of the Reading Room of the British Museum, an eminently "establishment" post in an eminently Bloomsbury institution, which had brought Wilson into contact with the world of what K. W. Gransden calls "English high culture":[2] scholarship, the Civil Service, universities, art galleries, and the B.B.C. If certain passages resemble C. P. Snow (for instance, the conversation between Bernard Sands and Charles Murley in book 1, chapter 5), it is not surprising: *Hemlock and After* is in part a novel about cultural officialdom by a cultural official.

But it is much more than this. Its title, with its reference to the condemnation and death of Socrates in 399 B.C., suggests Wilson's ambivalent feelings about the relationship between official authority and individual integrity; and its prose, though sometimes moving with old-fashioned leisureliness, embodies thoughts and sensations that seem to well up, as in Wilson's short stories, from a source deep in his instincts. Evelyn Waugh, who reviewed the novel in the Roman Catholic periodical the *Month,* perceptively described it as a "singularly rich, compact and intricate artifice."[3] While being carefully shaped as a series of set pieces, counterpointing different but interlocking attitudes and environments, it is full of details drawn from what Wilson calls "free memory,"[4] which give it the dense texture of reality.

In his Ewing lectures, published in 1963 as *The Wild Garden,* Wilson referred to novels as springing from "a momentary unified vision of life": they are, in essence, metaphors, extended in a particularly difficult medium (*WGa*, 149–50). He described the vision from which *Hemlock and After* originated as "a momentary powerful visual picture of a fat woman and a thin man." This was reproduced in the original opening of the novel[5] (paragraph 12 of the published version) as a "blurred glimpse" of the "elephant figure" of Vera Curry received by the thin man, the eminent novelist Bernard Sands, as his car "sped past" her vulgarly picturesque cottage. Before the novel opens, the two, both residents of Vardon, have been rivals for the possession of Vardon Hall, an old local house which Bernard has acquired as a Utopian retreat for artists and poets, and to which after long struggle he has persuaded the government to give financial support. During the novel's action, which covers a two- or three-month period in the summer of 1951, they are antagonists in a deeper sense, Bernard the liberal humanist, reasonable, responsible, and kind, at least by conviction and intention, and Mrs. Curry both self-indulgent and ruthless, imbued with sentimental notions of love which in fact enable her to profit from the weakness of others.

For Bernard, Mrs. Curry has become the focus for a "growing apprehension of evil" that has lately "begun . . . to disrupt his comprehension of the world."[6] As the novel progresses, his new unease turns him from the successful "Grand Old Man of Letters" into a self-accusing figure, unable to act clearly because of his perception of the complexity of human motives. The assumptions of *Hemlock and After,* which partially resembles a Greek tragedy, are not Christian ones; but Bernard's predicament is akin to that realized by Dean Jocelin, the cathedral-building hero of William Golding's *The Spire* (1964): "There is no innocent work." For a non-Christian liberal humanist such a recognition is more devastating.

The confident passage with which Wilson finally chose to open the novel seems intended to set Bernard on a narrow plateau of triumph, as he savors the message of financial support from the civil servant

Stephen Copperwheat, whose shrewdly chosen name exudes official smugness. Bernard's feelings, however, are a little complacent: the words "satisfaction" and "satisfied" occur no fewer than six times in the first two pages and suggest that Bernard's sense of security comes too easily. The third-person narrator, who at this point enters his character's thoughts, presents Bernard as experiencing only perfunctory self-doubt, which he is easily able to control: "if on occasion he mistrusted his own powers, it was not a mistrust he intended others to share" (*HA*, 11). The irony of this sentence is revealed (bk. 2, chap. 3) when Bernard is unable to make his intention good at the official opening of Vardon Hall. Meanwhile, as the reader senses the hubris in Bernard's understandable pleasure, the touch of self-congratulation in his stance as an "anarchic humanist" who delights in not filling the public role of eminent novelist, and as Bernard himself recognizes the neurotic withdrawal of his wife Ella, the hostility of his politically ambitious son James, the destructive malice of Mrs. Curry, and—even as he maneuvers skillfully in it—the alien world of right-wing "season-ticket gentry"[7] in the Home Counties, there seems nowhere for Bernard to go but down.

Approaching sixty, Bernard is something of a survival, with overtones of André Gide (who died the year the novel was written), Emile Zola[8] (on whom Wilson published a study in 1952), E.M. Forster (who in the 1920s had begun, as Bernard now begins, to wonder whether humanism "was a totally adequate answer", *HA*, 56), and perhaps also, in his slow elaboration of moral dilemmas, Henry James. Impatient with the quizzical Socratic method, or "pedantic bullying," that Bernard has followed as a parent, his son James has no truck with the literary critics' view of Bernard's books, a "gentle and ironic questioning of our most accepted values." Yet in their authoritarian attitude to society and their own children James and his wife Sonia are clearly not offered as viable alternatives, and their milieu—with its pseudo-chic talk of travel abroad, foreign food, and "in" writers—is fixed by Wilson's unblinking eye for cultural trendiness and described with what Stephen Wall has nicely summarized as a "sniper's precision and economy."[9]

The setting of his novel, too, shows Wilson's sharp awareness of the contemporary scene. Nineteen fifty-one was the year of the Festival of Britain, which opened on the South Bank of the Thames in London on 3 May. In book 1, chapter 1 Bernard's daughter Elizabeth and his former lover Terence Lambert visit the Dome of Discovery.

Among other things the Festival of Britain publicized and encouraged
the work of British artists and writers, and this provided Wilson with
a convenient outside frame of reference for Bernard's concept of Vardon Hall.[10] Nineteen fifty-one was also the last year in office of the
Labour government voted in in 1945; thus the novel's opposition of
left-oriented liberalism (Wilson's own inclination) and entrenched
"traditional" authority is backed by historical fact: 1951 as the last
flowering, or last gasp, of that prewar Fabian hopefulness of which
Bernard and Ella were a part.

Bernard's "position and authority" as a respected novelist has overcome official doubts as to whether Vardon Hall should be left to the
management of the writers themselves. But while, as a novelist, Bernard employs on society the Socratic, questioning method, he also,
like Socrates, "frequents by choice the society of lads of promise."[11]
Bernard is, in fact, despite his marriage and two children, homosexual by temperament and, more recently, by practice. Ella's neurotic
state, it is revealed much later, has been caused partly by her realization of this. Being a homosexual in England before the Wolfenden
Report led to the legalization of homosexual practices between con-
senting adults, Bernard is socially vulnerable, and for readers in 1952
the novel's courageous and remarkably unselfconscious presentation of
the precarious world of the homosexual was its most striking feature.

This world is introduced in the first part of book 1, chapter 2 (ap-
propriately called "Country Matters" after the use of that phrase in
Hamlet) by means of a casual meeting by St. Alban's Abbey between
Eric Craddock, a middle-class, good-looking would-be poet, and Ron
Wrigley, an example of the postwar cockney spiv. Both are protégés:
Eric is Bernard's lover, indulging in fantasies of himself as a page at
the court of Lorenzo di Medici while also "improving" himself under
Bernard's guidance; Ron, devoted to his sharp wardrobe of drape
suits, picks up a living by doing various jobs, with no questions
asked, for Mrs. Curry. Their encounter, alive to all the nuances of
homosexual "getting off," is inconclusive, its real purpose being to
suggest to the reader, in Dickensian fashion, the thin crust of respect-
ability on which Bernard's life as a public figure rests. Ron learns
from Eric of his friendship with Bernard, and in the latter part of the
chapter, depicting the horrible "cosiness," corrupt sentiment, and
sexual innuendo of Mrs. Curry's establishment, the information is
passed on. As Mrs. Curry, vast in her pink nightdress, has a psychic
version of Bernard and Ella ("their faces had such terrible looks of

misery, and, yes, you could only call it disgrace"; *HA,* 47), the reader feels a tremor of sympathetic foreboding.

In the next two chapters, moving forward in time only slowly, Wilson continues to build up, expanding sideways as if in parallel short stories, the detailed set pieces that present the totality of Bernard's complex life as famous novelist, husband, father, lover, brother, and friend. These aspects cannot always be kept separate. His daughter Elizabeth, who writes "bright" articles for a women's magazine, has recently heard hints of Bernard's homosexuality from the malicious theater producer Sherman Winter. Thus Bernard finds himself explaining to her his "selfish, but to me necessary, decision" to follow his homosexual inclinations, despite "possible harm" to his children: "Harm to others is after all implicit in most decisions we take, and has to be weighed up when taking them" (*HA,* 58). Bernard's past decisiveness, based on what he took to be an awareness of all the factors involved, is to contrast ironically with his state of indecision in book 2.

Bernard's loss of the will to act is to some extent prefigured in political terms (bk. 1, chap. 4) when he visits his sister Isobel, a professor of English devoted to left-wing political activities in which Bernard has shared in the past. Isobel has sensed in Bernard's recent work "an almost unreal religious quality," and he now refuses the request made by Isobel and her younger friend Louie Randall that he help them in a left-wing organization concerned to rally middle-class opinion about world peace. He chooses rather to hope that "good sense, or fear, or better still compassion will prevail." For Bernard, the simplicities of the past are no longer simple.

Bernard's crisis, where uncertainty about external situations is internalized into self-blame, occurs at the end of chapter 5. Bernard has taken Eric, whom he is trying to prize free from his mother's possessiveness, to a performance of Ibsen's *Ghosts;* during the interval Eric and Terence Lambert, with whom Bernard is still very friendly, have circled each other warily, and Sherman Winter—one of Bernard's embodiments of evil—has demonstrated his "camp" spite. The following day Bernard tries to persuade Terence not to "make for the nearest sewer" by going to live with Sherman, whose professional contacts Terence needs while disliking him personally. Failing in his first efforts, Bernard arranges to meet Terence later that night in Leicester Square on the edge of the Soho red-light district. Meanwhile, having met his old friend Charles Murley, now a civil servant at the Treasury, at a party, he dines with him, and during their subsequent discussion of the Vardon Hall scheme Bernard's satisfaction with his own "anarchic" impatience of government and university caution is contrasted, not altogether to his advantage, with Murley's feeling that, for all their faults, people like Copperwheat have only been guilty of "the simple and proper use of authority."

Afterwards, waiting for Terence in the "sheer ugliness" of Leicester Square, Bernard is approached by a young man who asks for a light: a solitary homosexual, Bernard immediately perceives. The young man is arrested by a lurking plainclothes policeman who also asks Bernard whether he wishes to make a complaint. The incident not only crystallizes for the reader the riskiness of homosexuality in an intolerant society, but also reveals to Bernard the uglier impulses that lurk beneath his liberalism and his feeling that, unlike Charles Murley, he has "kept his imagination free." As Terence bears him off in a taxi, Bernard realizes to his horror that, for however brief a moment, he sadistically enjoyed the "hopeless terror" in the arrested man's face—an enjoyment which the policeman, merely doing a job, did not share. Book 1 closes with two sentences heavy with reflexive sarcasm and cold with self-disgust:

Truly, he thought, he was not at one with those who exercised proper authority. A humanist, it would seem, was more at home with the wielders of the knout and the rubber truncheon. (*HA*, 107)

The rest of the novel, consisting of five chapters which symmetrically balance the first five, shows the effect of this scene on the remaining weeks of Bernard's life: a short, sharp heart attack, not presented directly but recounted by Terence to Elizabeth, is followed by the intermittent but progressive weakening of Bernard's will to act; its lowest point is reached after the fiasco of the official opening of Vardon Hall on a preternaturally hot Thursday in June. Bernard's decline is accompanied by the gradual resurrection of Ella, who finds in his need for her, and through some unexplained inner toughness which enables her to fight her neurosis, the power "to live again fully in the world around her." It is she, finally, who makes in Bernard's name the moral choices and practical decisions that his self-reproach inhibits him from making.

Convalescing at Vardon after his heart attack, Bernard watches Ella gardening and reflects bitterly that in her calm, automatic decisions about which plants to include and exclude, to nurture or uproot, she is displaying "the proper exercise of authority" in which he is no longer fitted to share. In bringing home his own implication in evil, the Leicester Square incident is to Bernard akin to Socrates' acquiescence in his condemnation by society for corruption of the young. The speech he makes at the opening of Vardon Hall represents the public drinking of the hemlock, as, instead of contributing to the success of the occasion by "a clear, humorous and high-minded speech," Bernard shares with a largely unsympathetic audience his doubts as to the motives of any human action:

Motives were so difficult, so double, so much hypocrisy might spring from guilt, so much benevolence from fear to use power, so much kindness overlay cruelty, so much that was done didn't matter. If the scheme failed, if the young writers ceased to write, it was of small account in time; better failure than deception, better defeat than a victory where motive was wrong. (HA, 151)

Wilson does not permit these sincere, though somewhat self-indulgent sentiments, which beget a mixture of sympathy and impatience in the reader, to set the prevailing tone in the multifaceted chapter entitled "Up at the Hall." This, a tour de force of satirical comedy and black farce, which recalls the short stories "Saturnalia" and "Totentanz," brings together for the opening of Vardon Hall all the different milieus on which Bernard impinges: from that of the Oxford don who quotes Pushkin to that of Sherman Winter and his "gay" friends who rampage "like mating mice" through the Hall's bedrooms and scandalize the local gentry, on down to Ron Wrigley and his drunken Dickensian mother who recommends rhubarb root to Celia Craddock as a specific for unwanted pregnancies. Building up premonition, and supplying afterthought, well in advance of Bernard's speech, Wilson presents the opening of Vardon as a chapter of accidents, misunderstandings, and malice, human and cosmic. The speech, confused though it is and laced with unintended sexual ambiguity, is for Bernard a crucial, self-destructive confession; but to Sonia it is "appalling bilge," to Charles Murley it is irresponsible "stinking fish," and to many of those listening outside through inefficient loudspeakers, it is garbled into "strange, sub-human explosions." The final chapters represent two sorts of aftermath. In book 3, chapter 1, entitled "In Sickness and in Health," Bernard and Ella suffer their separate, solitary hells of self-blame and neurosis, and emerge, Ella to help Bernard, Bernard to do as much as he feels his mixed motives entitle him to do about two situations that have been developing throughout the novel and have been tellingly juxtaposed in the chapter called "Life-loving Ladies."

The first involves Eric Craddock, whose emancipation from his clinging, histrionic but not totally unsympathetic mother was to have been brought about by a move to London, subsidized by Bernard. Apparently acquiescent in this, Celia Craddock has told Eric, with sweet and sickening "realism," that if he goes she will not be able to look after his beloved Muscovy ducks, the "Bolshies," which will have to be destroyed. Set back thus, Eric feels also deserted by Bernard, whose misgivings about his own motives have obliged him, while keeping his offer to help open, to stand back from Eric's course of action. A letter from Celia Craddock, a masterpiece of hypocritical high-mindedness, urging Bernard to withdraw completely, to be "cruel to be kind," reaches him after the Vardon opening and stirs in him a wish to act, though at first indirectly: "If he was to claim Eric from the net, he thought, he must release the other rabbit first" (*HA*, 202).

"The other rabbit" is a fifteen-year-old girl called Elsie Black, whom Mrs. Curry has procured to satisfy the regressive sexual tastes of Hubert Rose, an architect living at Vardon. The scene (in "Life-Loving Ladies") in which the arrangement is finalized between Mrs. Curry and Rose is presented with a sickliness of innuendo calculated to leave little room for sympathy with him: "He [Rose] understood his needs so well, and felt so deeply that they should be satisfied." Expecting Bernard to have a tolerance for compulsions akin to his own, Rose is both surprised and angry when Bernard, who has wormed the full details out of Ron Wrigley, tells him with dignity and firmness not to persevere with his plans.

The effect of Bernard's admonition is to bring Mrs. Curry on a reciprocal errand to Ella: Bernard, too, has habits that would not bear public scrutiny.[12] The discreet hints of blackmail are repudiated by Ella with a refreshing briskness and contempt. To Bernard, Mrs. Curry is a symbol of evil, to his brother-in-law Bill Pendlebury, in his sillier moments, she is a primitive matriarchal force, to her client/victims she is a powerful purveyor of expensive loans or illicit pleasures; but to Ella she is no more than "someone's cook dressed up" or "a new chair cover sent on approval."

The discussion between Ella and Bernard that follows Mrs. Curry's visit is the most moving passage in the novel, made so by its creaking, stilted air, a long-unused communication between two people who no longer respond to life with the same instincts. Yet Bernard's painful self-questioning and Ella's clarion call to action are alike admirable, as is their mutual admission of their past mistakes, and the chapter seems about to conclude with some return to vitality for Bernard, who feels acutely the reproaches about his apparent loss of faith in the Vardon Hall scheme which Charles Murley has uttered in letters to himself and Ella. It reaches, however, only as far as an apologetic letter to his sister Isobel, from whom he has parted coldly after the Vardon opening. "Exhausted with the program of common activity that lay before him," his "tattered humanism" is not sorry to succumb to a heart attack brought on by the mushroom omelette Ella has cooked for him—an ironic symbol, perhaps, of the unbridgeable gap between his regained decisiveness and his corrosive sense of life's complexity.

The epilogue is partly a tidying-up of ends left loose by Bernard's death, partly an illustration of what happens, for good or ill, when others take over his tasks. In one sense Bernard's death has long seemed inevitable, his concern about evil no more than a symptom of something deeper which dogs him: the heavy toll taken by the soul-searching inseparable from fully conscientious humanism. The loaded carefulness of the novel's prose reinforces one's feeling that Bernard's age is more like seventy than the fifty-seven ascribed to him, and K. W. Gransden's view that the speech at Vardon Hall expresses "the liberal-humanist death-wish"[13] is an acute one.

At the same time his death is a convenient simplicity of plot. Though he indicates convincingly to Ron Wrigley and Hubert Rose that he would not fear exposure in the course of bringing the latter to book, Bernard is, as he says to Ella, "not with the authority of the law." Indeed, had he taken his battles to the limit, the novel might have needed to grow an extra theme: the fight of the homosexual against a persecuting society, a subject treated in 1957 by the pioneering British film *Victim,* starring Dirk Bogarde. At the least, Bernard would have become the accessory of the official society he so much mistrusts.

The transference of Bernard's responsibilities to Ella avoids such complications, though the resultant "mass dealing out of justice" has its ironies. Ella pursues her hostility to the "perfectly foul" with a vigor that sends Mrs. Curry and Ron Wrigley to prison, and drives the arrested Hubert Rose to suicide, though the latter result is both unintended and regretted. "I wish," Ella sighs with a touch of Bernard's deeper compunction, "that one could act in single things without involving so many others. Such a lot of wicked things get mixed up with any good one does" (*HA*, 234–35). The latter remark has its bearing on Vardon Hall, placed by Charles Murley, of all people, in the charge of an efficient, money-saving administrator whose notions are by no means so repugnant to the young writers who live there as they would have been to Bernard. Neither Bernard nor Ella can long affect a world bound in other directions, nor people who lack the inner grace to benefit. As if to emphasize the temporariness of simplistic retribution, Mrs. Curry and Ron are shown putting their prison sentence to good use, strictly in their own terms: Mrs. Curry emerges after two years with "a most useful group of loving, dutiful girls through whom she could bring snugness and cosiness to respectably lonely gentlemen," and Ron finds the "monastic" prison community pleasantly responsive to his "old one two."

The conclusion of the novel, as Ella and Elizabeth fly off for a holiday, and Ella ponders the shortness of her own "doing" as against the eventual power for good of Bernard's "being," recedes into an equivalent authorial distance, a final ambiguity. Through showing Eric his mother's letter to Bernard, Ella has enabled him to break free of the silver cord: Eric's apprenticeship to Bernard gives him, in London, the perspicacity to reject the corny advances of an athletic parson and the maturity to attempt a rapprochement with his mother without ceasing to be himself. Terence, remembering Bernard's warnings, finds the strength to abandon his "kept" life with Sherman Winter and "take up his complicated fight alone once more." These, one may feel, are Bernard's posthumous victories of the spirit; but at what cost, and alongside what defeats, have they been won? Turning away, like Ella, from the confused world of action, the reader may also find it "easier to concentrate on the clouds moving above and below like great golden snowdrifts."

Hemlock and After is an impressive, exciting first novel, though not an altogether satisfactory one. It was recommended to its members by the Book Society, and most commentators have thought highly of it. In Wilson's own view it is "too truncated"[14] because written in only four weeks; but his admiration for the long novel[15] caused its comparative brevity to be packed with detail that, like an aggregation of short stories, substitutes suggestive vertical thickness for linear extension. This crowded texture is both a strength and a weakness. The differentiation of a sizable cast of characters by means of the minutiae of dialogue and description—Ella's images of neurosis, Mrs. Wrigley's sordid kitchen, Isobel's elegant choice of dishes for luncheon, the inn at Roddingham where Hubert Rose and Mrs. Curry meet, the haunted country walks taken by Bernard—is fascinating piece by piece, but the interrelationship of so many elements carries with it variations of emotional level and narrative stance that do not always match.

Whereas, for example, Bernard and Ella are seen in all their human complexity from within, Mrs. Curry, her brief "psychic" trances apart, is viewed from the outside, an embodiment of evil whom most critics have concurred in finding melodramatic and overdrawn: at different times and through different eyes, she resembles an intruder from the worlds of J. C. (and perhaps T. F.) Powys, D. H. Lawrence, and Joyce Cary. Though her presentation has some force in the novel, it combines somewhat unstably the embarrassing, the disgusting, and the would-be sinister. Bill Pendlebury's "accidental" overhearing of her arrangement for Hubert Rose is too convenient a contrivance; and the reader may also feel that Wilson, who betrays authorial bias *in propria persona* by referring to "the wretched Elsie Black" (*HA,* 216), is unduly harsh to Rose.[16]

Nevertheless, these are minor cavils at a novel that deals movingly with its important central subject, and that gives a total impression of great force and imaginative vitality. It was fairly summed up by J. D. Scott in the *New Statesman* as one of the three or four best novels he had read since the war,[17] a considerable achievement for a writer who described himself as "totally untutored when I wrote it."[18]

The Mulberry Bush

A less sympathetic, though not a hostile, picture of the limitations of liberalism is offered in Wilson's only stage play, which was first performed at the Bristol Old Vic in September 1955. It is possible to infer from the varied nature of his creative work in the early 1950s— a first novel, an amusing epistolary re-creation of the 1920s, *For Whom the Cloche Tolls* (1953), and this play—that Wilson had not made his final choice of literary medium. But though, after its publication, *The Mulberry Bush* was put on at the Royal Court Theatre in

London in April 1956, and televised in 1957, it did not succeed so well as to tempt him into further work for the stage, and after he retired from the British Museum in 1955 he concentrated his creative expression, with the exception of one book treated at the end of this chapter, on the writing of novels. If liberals of the same generation as Leonard and Virginia Woolf were a dying breed, so too, perhaps, were plays about them.

In *The Mulberry Bush* Wilson moves from the world of anarchic humanist writers to the drier one of liberal rationalist academics. The play, which in well-made play fashion covers the short period of two days and remains in the same location, concerns three generations of the Padley family, from James and Rose, in their seventies, to Ann and Simon, in their twenties, and among other things it gives fuller expression to a theme only touched on in *Hemlock and After:* the comparative failure of liberals as parents, whatever their achievements as, in this case, enlightened historians and social workers. The mulberry bush (or tree) of the title stands in the garden of the senior Padley's home, the Master's Lodge of an Oxbridge college.[19] The bush is described in a stage direction as "distorted and strangely shaped," with some of its roots held by "iron bands," a symbol of family continuity both in a positive and a negative sense. Lying under it in act 2, the drunken Simon, tired of his do-gooding atheistic Padley heritage but unable to break free from it, mockingly varies a line from the old song: "Here we go round the bloody mulberry bush."

The precarious position of the liberal in postwar society is suggested by what is presented in act 1: the retirement of James Padley and his replacement as Warden by a businesslike administrator, Sir Peter Heppell. James is hoping that his assistant, a young historian called Peter Lord, will stay on under the uncongenial new dispensation to represent "decent, liberal-minded people," but first accompany him to Harvard, where he is to lecture and hopes to speak out against the McCarthyite witch-hunting of American academic friends. Peter, however, feels that James will fail and only hurt himself, and at the end of the play his resistance to doing what James wants of him hardens: he accepts a government job that will satisfy both his working-class ambitions and his wish to exert an influence for good on the teaching of history. How he will do this is not clear, nor whether he is really interested in much more than "careers and pushing," as Ann Padley thinks in act 1. But as, after thinking herself in love with her mixed-up cousin Simon, Ann finally agrees to marry Peter, Wilson presumably is implying that the younger Padley stock

needs strengthening and that Peter is the nearest thing to a contin-
uator of Padley ideals. What he offers Ann is "a useful full life" instead of "gentle pathos . . . rainsoaked melancholy."[20]

These attitudes have been induced in Ann by the revelations of act
2, which have upset her previous simple admiration of her father,
Robert Padley, a famous humanist and social worker prematurely
dead when the play begins. He functions in the play like the hole at
the center of a whirlpool, toward the emptiness of which the beliefs
of the living Padleys are sucked, as a result of what they learn about
him. In spite of Rose Padley's assertion in act 3 that "the people and
the facts remain the same," Wilson demonstrates again, as in *Hemlock
and After,* the vulnerability of humanism when confronted with what,
in another context of belief, would seem the likely backslidings of
ordinary, sinful human nature.

Geraldine Laughton-Moore is the first revelation. Despite an apparently happy marriage, Robert has had a mistress, who wishes after
his death to meet his daughter. The senior Padleys try to prevent
this, and in doing so (Peter Lord, significantly, objects) they reveal
the managing, patronizing element that accompanies their liberal beliefs; they are too sure they know best. In act 2, set in the garden,
a location designed to suggest the presence in life of "old powers and
magics" which the senior Padleys cannot control and try to deny,
Geraldine arrives anyway, summoned by a telegram. She reveals to
Ann not only that her father needed the love of an unjudging "sensitive" woman, but also that, though to all appearances inheriting the
high-minded atheism of his parents, he was afraid of dying and went
to séances. At the end of the act she pronounces: "young people
shouldn't live among ruins" (*MB,* 86), which is also Peter Lord's
view, reached by a different route.

Before this, and adding to the force of what she says, Captain Walcott, an ex-First World War officer, has arrived and revealed further
details about Robert's life. Walcott, apparently knowingly, has been
used by Robert, whom he still calls "the great man," as a scapegoat
for something that happened twenty-five years before at the start of
Robert's career: a brief affair with a girl at a mixed camp which he
ran. Walcott, who lost his job and is now a door-to-door salesman,
did not blame Robert, who "had everything to give the world and I
had nothing" (*MB,* 80). Nevertheless, Ann and the audience judge
more harshly: Walcott's life has been spoiled by the slur, and Robert,
to whom the claims of personal relations should have mattered, has

exploited his friend's admiration in order to protect his own public image.

The information furnished by Geraldine and Captain Walcott cannot fail to have its effect on the Padley menage, but the mechanisms that bring them into it are too theatrically convenient, even though they stem from a malice located in the two characters by whom they are summoned. Geraldine is invited by Wendy Tellick, a neurotic young woman in love with Simon, who hopes to prize him away from Ann; Walcott, met in a pub, is invited by Kurt Landeck, a German-Jewish refugee whom Rose Padley has in effect adopted. Both are "lame dogs" who have received kindness from the older Padleys and are credibly ungrateful. Neither is pleasant, yet both illustrate attitudes not automatically to be set aside. Wendy is right-wing, racist, and tends to overvalue emotion; but when she criticizes Simon, and by implication the Padley household, for "talking not feeling" (*MB*, 59), she is far from wrong. Her opposite number, Kurt Landeck, though he exploits his position as a refugee to gain sympathy and is treated by Rose Padley as a little boy, is more than a mere Peter Pan. His parasitism is accompanied by intelligence and a ruthlessness learned from Nazi Germany. One feels that he is aware of a nasty area of human experience beside which the Padleys' liberalism seems a pious fantasy. Squeezed between the twin totalitarianisms of Nazism and Communism, the Padleys' beliefs, though Wilson sympathizes with them, have a pathetic air. Kurt's final decision to attach himself to the new world of the Heppells both disappoints and disabuses them, but it is understandable.

In act 3 Kurt recites, mockingly, the Padley virtues and faults:

"Tolerance, pity, courage, learning—how does it go on? Patronage, interference, pushing people around, patting oneself on the back." (*MB*, 100)

The virtues are really there, though we are not sure about tolerance: Geraldine Loughton-Moore's name is chosen by Wilson so as to show Rose Padley being snobbish: "Genteel artiness! And down at heels at that! She probably cost Robert a fortune in awful curio shops or badly-run snack bars" (*MB*, 27). The Padleys too easily assume a patronizing manner, setting aside people whose habits differ from their own; even in act 3 Rose still speaks of Ann's decision to marry Peter in these brisk and automatic terms: "All this business about marrying Peter will probably blow over. He's a fine man, but he's not what we intended . . . We must find her something useful to do" (*MB,* 109). Responsive to people as social problems and statistics, Rose is slow to see they have lives of their own, and as even her well-disposed daughter, Cora Fellowes, points out in act 1, sex, love, and passion, ignored in her upbringing, are elements in human nature, as well as the impulse to do others good.

At the end of the play, among their packing-cases, both Padleys have realized that they "belong to the past." Rose's reaction, shadowed by despair, is nevertheless indomitable: she can only go on doing what she does best, and the curtain falls on her as she annotates a government document. James Padley, a retiring figure for most of the play, emerges in an attempt to communicate with his wife on the personal level, but fails. Their marriage has never involved great emotional closeness, and he is left "a broken man," feeling obscurely that he has failed as a father. As in *Hemlock and After,* Wilson's mixture of affection for, and reservations about, the liberal mentality produces an ambiguous and chastened conclusion.

The Mulberry Bush is far from lacking in merit. Its dialogue is crisp, its characters efficiently contrasted to demonstrate the different values seething uncertainly after World War II. There are some effective theatrical moments, particularly the argument between Peter Lord and Landeck in act 1, in which positive and negative types of ruthlessness strike sparks from each other. Kurt Landeck's slightly stilted German English is an impressive example of Wilson's ear for speech forms, and Landeck is perhaps the most interesting character in the play: a study of selfish drive that balances Rose Padley's absorption in abstract altruism. In terms of character, James Padley is the play's weak point: he never projects a definite sense of his convictions, so that his feeling of defeat at the end seems more melodramatic than involving. The dialectical method of dialogue does not, by itself, allow Wilson to express the full humanity of his characters; beside Ella Sands, Rose Padley is a skeleton, and Simon and Wendy come over as stagy embodiments of cynicism and neurosis. There are, also, too many emotional twists and turns, too many attacks reversed by an urge to be fair to all viewpoints, too many different moments of "dramatic" confrontation, to allow the play to articulate its theme with either sufficient force or a sufficiently moving depth of bewilderment.

Nor does the play break altogether new dramatic ground. In its reliance on the conventions of the "well-made play" it resembles the work of Terence Rattigan, and in its subject, though not in its treatment, it resembles a popular, far less "intellectual" play, J. B. Priestley's similarly titled *The Linden Tree* (1948), which had already dealt with the predicament of a professor of history, on the point of retirement, surviving into a world inimical to his long-cherished ideals. With the coming of John Osborne's *Look Back in Anger,* performed at the Royal Court Theatre in 1956, a few weeks later than *The Mulberry Bush,* a new period began in English drama, one in which neither Wilson's concern with liberalism, nor its upper-middle-class exponents, would feel at home.

A Bit off the Map (1957)

Wilson's second novel, *Anglo-Saxon Attitudes,* appeared in 1956. The comparative failure of *The Mulberry Bush,* published and reperformed in the same year, left his career temporarily hanging fire, since he did not yet have another novel ready. As an expedient, his publishers suggested he produce another volume of short stories, and in order to bring this up to a reasonable length he sequestered himself in a hotel in order to write some new ones. The result is that the eight stories of his third volume, *A Bit off the Map,* published the following year, are equally divided between new work and old, so that it lacks the coherence of his two earlier volumes. Only of some of the specially written ones, all set in 1955-1956, does the description hold that Wilson gave in an interview published in 1957: they are "satirical of the old philosophies that have now become fashionable again—neo-Toryism, Colin Wilson's Nietzscheanism, and so on—of people seeking after values which no longer apply."[21] As 1951 was the end of left-wing hopefulness, so 1956, the year of Britain's unsuccessful part in the Suez crisis, was the end of right-wing authority and imperial possessiveness.

The four earlier stories, set in the 1940s, are more sympathetic to the various predicaments of their characters. "A Flat Country Christmas," originally published in the *New Statesman* on Christmas Day 1950 under the title of "The Old Old Message," is set among the purpose-built bungalows and few remaining older houses of a "New Town" in 1949. Remembering at Christmas the old-fashioned parents they feel thankful to have escaped, the two dissimilar but friendly young couples, "tolerant, forward-looking, never anti-social," nevertheless conceal only just below the surface fears of the atom

bomb, fears of getting stuck where they are, and, in Ray's final horrified vision in a mirror rigged up to serve as a crystal ball, a sense of
nothingness looming in the future. In "Once a Lady," first published
in the *New Yorker* and set in a north Midlands village just after the
war, Esther Barrington lives with the consequences of a rebellious
love-match to her lower-class husband. Years later, the love still exists but her life has been worn down to a succession of dreary, repet-
itive tasks in a limited environment, with only one middle-class
friend, the bluff, lesbian-inclined Eileen Carter, with whom to recapture something of her former self. What horrifies her particularly is
the possibility, suggested by Eileen in momentary malice but then
withdrawn in the phrase of the story's title ("Once a lady, always a
lady"), that she is now virtually indistinguishable from her working-
class neighbors. In "Higher Standards," the shortest story, social mobility works the other way round. Elsie Corfe, a local school teacher,
has lost a natural sense of belonging to her environment through having had a better education than her former classmates, the "Standard
IV" she once belonged to. The inference is that her "Higher Standards," at once prized and resented, will prevent her from marrying
anybody available in her narrow community.

All these stories capture sharply the false positions people find
themselves in as a result of the processes of social change. The other
early story, "A Sad Fall," set in Shropshire in the last year of the war,
offers another version of liberal humanism (here seen in terms of the
value placed on the unique individual life) encountering the chilliness
of a more statistical approach. Mrs. Tanner, aged seventy, is entertaining John Appleby, a thirty-two-year-old mathematics lecturer at
Oxford and friend of her son. Enjoying his company, Mrs. Tanner
describes John as "so gentle in a violent, hurrying world," to which
he answers: "I shouldn't put so much trust in a world of gentleness
again." When Roger, a thirteen-year-old evacuee at her house, plays
a game of "spies" on the roof and falls through the greenhouse, severely injuring himself, both she and John rush to help, she with
warm solicitude, he with cool but concerned practicality. Nevertheless, to John, Roger is "a very ordinary boy" whose death would not
really "matter," as there are plenty like him. The view inspires Mrs.
Tanner, a diabetic, with an "irrational" fear for herself in a world of
such clinical detachment. This is a "sad fall" from innocence and
from human feeling. Though John is not presented as a monster—he
gets on well with Roger—and though there is some selfish sentimen-

tality in Mrs. Tanner's shocked reaction to his statements, it is fairly clear that Wilson's sympathies lie with the old lady.

Three of the remaining stories, the ones which Wilson wrote specifically for the volume and set in immediately contemporary Britain, differ from his usual practice in being very long and, essentially, concentrated on a single individual, almost as if Wilson had adopted the more leisurely approach of his recently published *Anglo-Saxon Attitudes*. Indeed, "After the Show," unique in Wilson's work until *Setting the World on Fire* in describing the mentality and milieu of a well-to-do, imaginative adolescent, was originally twice as long: Wilson published only its second half. It concerns a seventeen-year-old called Maurice Liebig, third generation of a nouveau-riche Jewish family, who returns with his grandmother from a performance of Ibsen's *The Wild Duck* to find himself thrust into a "real-life" situation that is uncannily like a play. His uncle's young mistress Sylvia's attempt at suicide is partly belied by her attention-seeking histrionics as she protests that life is meaningless. A brief rapport between them springs up, but seeing her the following day in a less romantic environment (recalling the Passion Fruit Club in "The Wrong Set"), he hastily extricates himself from a situation he is too young to handle, accompanying his grandmother, this time, to her choice, the musical *The Pajama Game*. It is, for Wilson, a most unusual type of story, and handled with great skill: a study both touching and humorous of a young man hesitating on the verge of life, caught between wish and fear, dream and reality.

Wilson keeps at a slight distance from Maurice by using the authorial third person. In the other two long stories he performs a tour de force of mimicry, inventing a first-person voice that both narrates the story and reveals the character of the narrator. "More Friend Than Lodger" is unique among his short stories in employing the first-person method throughout, though June Raven's habit of anticipating the reader's criticism by over-explaining herself perhaps betrays Wilson's lack of trust in the ability of her quasi-ingenuous style to tell its own story of her foibles. When not directly self-revealing, however, June's voice has an engaging wit, as when, talking of her husband Henry's admiration for Lady Ann Denton, she says:

"She's a sort of tarty substitute mother-figure for him, I think; and indeed, if he wanted a tarty mother, he had to find a substitute."[22]

June's style of speech makes her sound sometimes like a much more intelligent Louie, the narrator of that eminently 1920s classic, Anita Loos's *Gentlemen Prefer Blondes;* the verve of her mischievous behavior suggests a less destructive version of Lady Susan, the "heroine" of Jane Austen's epistolary first novel.

June's mischief, provoked by boredom with security, is first exercised against her dull publisher husband, by means of an affair with Rodney Galt, a handsome, ambitious author whose snobbery conceals origins that June's shrewdness is quick to spot. This "confidence-trickster" element does not disturb her *nostalgie de la boue;* what does is Rodney's getting serious and seeming to need her, since the key to June is that she is a "tease," flirting with risk but reverting to security if a really serious demand for commitment is made on her. At the end, Rodney as well as Henry suffers her mischief, when she leaks to a gossip column items calculated to embarrass them both, among them a reference to Rodney as "more friend than lodger" in the Raven household. How far one is meant to think of this as revenge for her disappointment, or to take seriously warnings given at different times by both Rodney and Henry that she will one day go "off her head" if she doesn't curb her brittle bitchiness, it is hard to tell. Her view of herself throughout is simply: "I don't really believe that one can't have one's cake and eat it." Yet behind her façade she does harbor the opinion that "life is, indeed, a cheat."

This, finally, is also the view of Kennie Martin, the protagonist of the title story "A Bit Off the Map." This was probably the most striking story for readers in 1957; it was certainly the most topical, presenting the England of coffee-bars and Teddy Boys. The method Wilson uses to tell the story is the same as that of "Necessity's Child" in *Such Darling Dodos:* two framing sections offering the thoughts of Kennie Martin, a twenty-one-year-old layabout (who isn't very strong) and psychopath (who doesn't know his own strength), and a central section describing in the third person "the Crowd"—a group of anti-humanist, Nietzschean, young would-be writers—and their milieu. The change of approach is partly to allow Wilson's satirical eye for "the Crowd" freer play than Kennie's severely limited intelligence would permit, and partly to show Kennie from the outside, flashy in his clothes and with a "foolish and beautiful" pale face, "a mixture" in the eyes of the aspiring young literary hostess Clara Turnbull-Henderson "of John Keats and cretinism."

Within Kennie's mixed-up brain, however, burns an obscure wish for "the Truth": for this reason he has become attached to Huggett, the leader of the group, whom he venerates. Drunk at Clara's party, he listens to a conversation between Huggett and the established critic Tristram Fleet, who regards Huggett's view of madness as a key to truth as "banal and tedious." Huggett's words exactly suit Kennie's need: metaphorical references—which Kennie takes literally—to "maps," "salvation," and "the Defence of the Realm Act." Later that night he encounters a harmless lunatic called Colonel Lambourn, who thinks he has found "the Truth" through maps of old bridle paths, listed Treasure Trove, and government defense zones: when superimposed the maps reveal "pentacles" containing something he calls "the putative treasure." At first Kennie is excited, thinking he has found "the Truth" where Huggett has said it could be found, "in Bedlam with Billy Blake"; but finally realizing that Lambourn is no more than a crank, programmed to deliver and repeat a message that makes no sense, Kennie screams out "It's a bloody cheat" and hits the old man violently in the face, leaving him unconscious. It is a neat ironic conclusion, with Kennie, as it were, the monster to Huggett's Frankenstein, and Wilson's not unsympathetic attempt to get inside Kennie's mind at the beginning is an interesting technical experiment. But one is not quite sure of the story's point: the Crowd's doctrines are half-baked enough, but Kennie's weak head would surely be likely to scramble anyone's doctrine.

The final story, "Ten Minutes to Twelve," takes place in the closing minutes of 1955. Lord Peacehaven, formerly Henry Biggs, is writing a memorandum to the firm of which he is chairman. It is couched in a style of confident, old-fashioned paternalism and recommends "action" as the firm's future watchword. We then discover that Peacehaven has been more or less mad since the New Year of 1935, and the firm has passed into others' control and survived into a more complicated age of technical expertise and delicate labor relations, in which "courage and individualism and high-handedness" have no place. Hearing the memorandum read out by Peacehaven's disapproving son Walter, his teen-age grandson Geoff dismays his assembled family by declaring approval of its authoritarian decisiveness. For him it is better to order people about "if they get in the way and don't pull their weight"; it is better than being "flat and dull and having good reasons for doing nothing." It is hard not to sympathize with Geoff's wish to bring in "a year of adventure and action," but ironically, the year is 1956, the year of Suez. "Adventure and action" seem to be the province only of the simple, unthinking young or those in the peaceful haven of old age and/or madness.

Some of the stories in *A Bit off the Map* extend Wilson's human territory and his technical range. But their recurrent motifs—the isolation of human beings from each other, their inability to cope with the postwar world, their occasional descents into the extreme introversion of madness—are not, on the whole, imbued with the fierceness and intensity found in Wilson's first two volumes of short stories. Written, or assembled, virtually to order, the stories, in general, possess neither a certainty of aim nor a tense and complex ambiguity. After *A Bit off the Map* Wilson wrote only a few short stories, including a monologue "Live and Let Die" (a phrase used by Ella Sands in *Hemlock and After*), and, after a visit to South Africa in 1961, an ironic comment on that country called "No Future for our Young." All have remained unpublished.

Chapter Four
Mid-life Crises

Retirement, in 1955, from his post at the British Museum allowed Angus Wilson scope to move from admiring the long novel of Victorian days to trying a novel of a similar kind himself. His earliest notes for what became *Hemlock and After* had projected a novel in four books and twenty-two chapters, to be called *Power and Affection,* of which only one paragraph appears to have survived. Such a novel would have been twice the size of *Hemlock and After,* and Wilson's second novel, *Anglo-Saxon Attitudes* (1956), is almost exactly this, though its material is differently subdivided. In place of the four weeks spent on *Hemlock and After,* four months were taken up with *Anglo-Saxon Attitudes;* in his *Paris Review* interview in 1957, Wilson said that "an awful lot of that time was taken up just with thinking."[1] The existence of five preliminary notebooks for the novel reinforces Wilson's statement, and in *The Wild Garden* he referred to *Anglo-Saxon Attitudes* rather disparagingly as "the most 'thought' of my novels and the least 'felt.' " (*WGa,* 131).

In fact, the element of conscious authorial thought in no way restricts the power of *Anglo-Saxon Attitudes* to keep the reader interested, and its successor of 1958, the slightly longer and more "felt" *Middle Age of Mrs. Eliot* had a sufficiently cool reception from some reviewers, and from some critics writing later, to make Wilson's value-distinction between thought and feeling difficult to accept. Nevertheless, despite the difference in their flavors and in the response they have provoked, the two novels have in common a basic situation, that of the individual confronted with a crisis and gradually coming to terms with it, a situation announced in *Hemlock and After* but sidestepped by Bernard's death.

The different forms taken by the crisis—in *Anglo-Saxon Attitudes* the hero's necessary plunge into the past for self-examination and the purging of the will, in *The Middle Age of Mrs. Eliot* the brutally unexpected change of the heroine from protected wifehood to exposed widowhood—may both be felt to reflect Wilson's personal situation in the mid-1950s, since he had abandoned a "safe" job in exchange

for the precarious life of the writer, alone with his wits and his memories, and had also moved, though not completely, from the sociabil-
ities of London to the East Anglian countryside. "What am I?" and
"How am I to proceed?" seem likely questions for a forty-three-year-
old writer to ask at such a juncture, and in part to explore through
fictional characters.

Anglo-Saxon Attitudes

The action of *Anglo-Saxon Attitudes,* like that of *Hemlock and After,*
takes place in Wilson's current present: over a period of one year beginning, with appropriate historical precision, on 22 December
1954. Unlike its shorter predecessor, however, which contented itself
with brief references-back to amplify the character of Bernard Sands,
Anglo-Saxon Attitudes reaches deeply into the past:[2] not only to 1912,
where its protagonist's story, and his mistakes, really begin, but also,
by means of the quasi-documentary of its preamble and appendices,
as far back as the time of the imaginary missionary Bishop Eorpwald,
who brought Christianity to East Anglia in the seventh century.[3]

Wilson's use of 1912 is no accident. Much of the novel's fascination is due to its being not only an analysis of its hero, Gerald Middleton—whose name suggests his position midway between the past
and the future, both personal and public—but also a piece of "historical" detective fiction with a real analogue. The key theme of the
novel, indicated in Wilson's notes, is "The Truth," and the truth
that Gerald faces and acts on applies to his own character as well as
to the community of history scholars to which he belongs; but the
plot framework Wilson derived for its expression was suggested to
him by the notorious "Piltdown man" hoax, which is mentioned
twice in the novel. It was in 1912, at Pilt Down near Uckfield in
Sussex, that the "discovery" was made of a skull that was taken to be
the hundred-and-fifty thousand-year-old "missing link" between apes
and men. In 1953 it was found to be a fraud, deliberately placed,
consisting of the jaw of a modern ape added to fragments of a genuine
ancient human skull.

Wilson's Piltdown, which leads to so many contorted "Anglo-
saxon attitudes" among the novel's many characters, is the "Melpham
Burial" whose discovery is announced in an imitation column from
the *Times* of November 1912, which precedes Part 1. The long-
sought-for tomb of Bishop Eorpwald has been discovered, at Melpham in Norfolk, by the local antiquarian Canon Portway and the

eminent medievalist Professor Lionel Stokesay; in the tomb, however, they have found a pagan phallic figure. At the end of the novel an appendix of quasi-factual extracts and reviews demonstrates the latter discovery. Portway uses it to emphasize the reliability of local tradition, which had preserved rumors that Eorpwald had backslid from Christianity. Stokesay admits the backsliding but treats it as an unimportant aberration: it does not diminish the greater importance of the Christianity brought from Rome as compared with that surviving in the Celtic church. Stokesay's pupil Rose Lorimer takes the discovery as a support for her romantic preference for the Celtic church, as well as for the notion that early Christianity in Britain was mixed with pagan elements. Professor Clun thinks Rose Lorimer a crank. All to a greater or lesser extent are wrong: a final extract, from the *Times* of 1955, reveals that the phallic fertility figure, though itself genuine, was planted in Eorpwald's tomb as a malicious practical joke by Stokesay's son Gilbert. Stokesay and Portway had guessed the truth by the 1920s but failed to admit it.

Despite the potential for mockery and farce inherent in the circumstances of the Melpham Burial, Wilson's treatment of the "history" element is both serious and engrossing. There is nothing in *Anglo-Saxon Attitudes*[4] (except perhaps at the end, when Rose Lorimer swings her shopping bags at the shins of Father Lavenham as she emerges from the British Museum) akin to the comic undermining of historians in Kingsley Amis's *Lucky Jim,* which had appeared two years earlier. Doubtless basing his depiction on the behavior of scholars observed from his vantage point in the British Museum Reading Room, Angus Wilson has produced, in the just summary of G.S. Fraser:

the only English novel . . . . which brings the dry, prickly, tetchy, and yet at its best, honorable, disinterested, and self-sacrificing world of learned societies and research in the humanities imaginatively alive.[5]

The novel's preamble and appendices, which are not parodies but clever imitations produced in the interests of greater verisimilitude, enclose the long and intricate story of how the falsehood of 1912 is transformed into the truth of 1955 by means of the belated quest of one particular historian, the recently retired Oxford Professor Gerald Middleton, author of the standard book on Cnut (Canute) and once an inspiring teacher, but also a rich and cushioned art collector who is described at the opening of Part 1 as having a "mildly but persistently depressive temperament." Gerald's depression proceeds from a sense, despite the respect in which he is held by fellow-historians of all ages, of personal and professional failure. Reading a newspaper exposé by his ex-M.P. son John of a case involving a civil servant called Pelican and a small market gardener called Harold Cressett, Gerald detests its sensationalist, ombudsman-cum-muckraker manner, but reflects immediately that, with his wealth and privilege, he has yet made too little of his own life to have the right to judge. What is he himself but "a sixty year old failure, and of that most boring kind, a failure with a conscience."[6]

At sixty-four,[7] reluctant to accept the editorship of the projected *Medieval History* that Sir Edgar Iffley and his own former students are urging on him, Gerald finds himself increasingly reminded, by various small circumstances, of two things he has particularly tried to suppress: "Dollie and Melpham! The two forbidden subjects of his thoughts." The two are connected, and as Part 1 unfolds it becomes clear that Melpham is at the root of his unwillingness to accept the editorship, and that his failure, years before, to marry Dollie (who later marries, and in World War I is widowed by, Gilbert Stokesay) accounts for his unsatisfactory relationship with his grotesque, whimsical Danish wife Inge, whom he has married on the rebound.

Somewhat in the manner of Dicken's *Bleak House,* where everything is related to the case of Jarndyce versus Jarndyce, *Anglo-Saxon Attitudes* is a complex web with Gerald at the center; not only Melpham, but the Pelican/Cressett case drags on throughout the novel, the latter intersecting with Gerald not only through the involvement of his son John but because Harold Cressett's "wooden," sinister wife, Alice, turns out to have entered Gerald's life on the very same afternoon in 1912 when he first met Dollie. The effect of such interconnections in the novel is to suggest, not the workings of mere coincidence, but the overlapping of human lives and the inescapable relationship of past and present—in short, the inevitability of history. It was presumably with *Anglo-Saxon Attitudes* in mind that Wilson spoke in 1957 of his effort to convince the reader of fictional "truth" by trying "to multiply the worlds I put into the book—so that, like the ripples of a stone thrown into the brook, you feel the repercussions going further and further out." For Wilson, as for Proust, "the strangest and most unlikely lives are in fact interdependent."[8]

Anglo-Saxon Attitudes is a very symmetrical novel, each of its two books being roughly equal in length, and each culminating in a decision vital to Gerald's future as a man and as a historian, and expressive of stages in his return to resilience and professional self-respect. This structural symmetry, however, is imposed on widely differing amounts of contemporary action by means of contrasting fictional techniques. Whereas Book 2 is a linear narrative covering about eleven months in 1955, Book 1 deals in great breadth and depth with only three days at the end of 1954. In terms of its approach to its material, the novel could have been entitled "Truth and Consequences."[9]

The intercommunications between the different elements of Gerald's past and present life are established in Book 1 by various easily recognizable, but nevertheless effective devices. In chapters 1 and 2 the links are lateral, somewhat in the manner of Virginia Woolf, and suggest the simultaneity of human existences. Chapter 1 is concerned with Gerald's professional environment, presenting in sequence his colleagues and pupils: the eccentric yet sympathetic Rose Lorimer; Gerald's anti-type, the pedantic Professor Clun (whose name is not the only thing about him that recalls the great Latinist A.E. Housman); the young lecturers Jasper and Theo, who feel, correctly, that only if Gerald accepts the editorship of the *Medieval History* will he regain the necessary energy to complete his long-delayed life of Edward the Confessor; Sir Edgar Iffley, grand old man of medievalists, who functions in the novel as the touchstone of historical integrity and human judgment (only once, in his view of Professor Clun at the end, is he declared by Wilson to be in error); and Professor Pforzheim, whose news in chapter 2 that a pagan figure has been found at the site of Aldwin's tomb in Heligoland introduces into the novel the idea that knowing the truth about Melpham, so long ago, may be essential to the historical research of the present.

A similar method is used in chapter 3, which juxtaposes Gerald and his sons—John the journalist, Robin who has taken over the Middleton steel-construction business whence Gerald's independent income derives—with remoter people and groups—Frank Rammage, the Cressetts, Lilian Portway and her companion Stephanie Houdet—who are to prove important later. Each section, from that describing Gerald's visit to his former charwoman, the Dickensianly named Mrs. Emma Adeline Salad, to that showing the whimsical paganism of Christmas Eve at his wife Inge's house in Marlow, contains the mention of a character who emerges more fully in the next. The effect is not merely to convey the coexistence of many contemporary, disparate life-styles, but also to link present and past: a person who in one world is merely remembered turns out still to exist, elsewhere, in another; or if not always that, to have left a surviving contemporary. For instance, Canon Portway is now only a memory to his former protégé Frank Rammage, a landlord in Earl's Court; but in Merano in the Italian Tyrol Portway's sister-in-law, the once great actress Lilian, is still living, aged seventy; her granddaughter Elvira Portway is both John Middleton's secretary and Robin Middleton's mistress.

Chapter 4, the longest in Book 1, repeats the "linked phrase" method of chapter 1 to extend Gerald's world backwards by means of a series of nine flashbacks, each one taking Gerald further into the past and, almost in the manner of deep Freudian analysis, closer to the historical roots of his present unease. Wilson's method is, of course, an authorial convenience: how many overheard conversations are likely to press so many buttons of memory, and in such neat chronological order? But it works in the context. Alienated in all but good manners from his unhappy, sentimental, managing wife, unable to communicate with even his loved daughter Kay whose burnt, withered hand is another mystery of his past, feeling that "his whole life had grown pale and futile because it was rooted in evasion," and sitting with brandy and coffee after a large Christmas dinner, Gerald in a doze of heightened consciousness is wafted in and out of half-forgotten scenes by phrases spoken by members of his family.

Prompted by a phrase of Robin's, "the wider truth of the situation the country's in," Gerald's memory returns first to Lionel Stokesay in 1938, two years before his death. Having involved himself in the policies of appeasement, and about to set off for the Dresden conference, seen by Gerald as "a Nazi government stunt" (*ASA,* 111), Stokesay has left behind the world of responsible historical scholarship, replacing it by a "a growing distaste for accuracy, a wider and wider canvas" (*ASA,* 113). The spectacle of his former teacher turning into a "gas balloon" planted in Gerald that distrust of the "wider implications" of history that has prevented him from using all his gifts as a historian.

The flashbacks, presented with great vividness, take Gerald through phases of his relationships with Dollie and with Inge. The reverse order forces the painful story to emerge in tantalizing puzzle-pieces, but it is clear that his mistress Dollie, for whom Gerald cared deeply and from whom in the 1920s he gained the assurance "to sustain the scope of his long work on Cnut," had had to be sacrificed to the distasteful responsibilities of his marriage. Ironically, the "protective calm" that Gerald saw in Inge in 1918 as an antidote to Dollie's "passion" and "tension" has turned into a bovine whimsy: their marriage has failed totally and they have ended up living apart. It seems that lack of courage has prevented Gerald from achieving either happiness in romance or satisfaction in domestic duty, and the strains of balancing family and mistress are embodied in vignettes set in Aigues-Mortes in 1932 and at the Café Royal in London in 1928. In these, Gerald's inability to communicate with his children, particularly with Kay, comes across sharply. He has never been able to discover how Kay's hand came to be badly burnt when she was a small child: was it an accident or did Inge cause it? Inge's hysterical distress at being questioned provoked such "physical nausea" in Gerald that ever since he has acquiesced in the atmosphere of childish sentimentality built up by Inge around herself, while putting himself at a disgusted distance from it.

Kay's hand is Gerald's family mystery. His professional one emerges in the last two flashbacks, triggered by John Middleton's phrase "moment of truth." Gerald first recalls a conversation with Gilbert Stokesay in a Soho restaurant in 1914. Gilbert, a ruthless Nietzschean who exults in the outbreak of war, writes avant-garde poems, and is linked by Wilson with the magazine *Blast,* looks down on Gerald as a "civilized bourgeois" who lacks the courage to seduce Dollie, now Gilbert's wife. Gilbert drunkenly boasts that he himself put the phallic figure in Eorpwald's tomb, out of contempt for his father's "scholarship." Despising his father's gullibility, he plans to "spill the beans" if ever his father gets a knighthood; instead, he himself is killed in action. Though momentarily convinced that Gilbert is telling the truth, Gerald later dismisses the story as one of Gilbert's frequent practical jokes. He has never revealed it: if true, its truth is both too unimportant in itself and too important in terms of its possible human repercussions. The final flashback, describing Gerald's visit to the Portways' home at Melpham in 1912, as a handsome, just-graduated brilliant student of Lionel Stokesay's, suggests slight oddities in the circumstances of the discovery of Eorpwald's tomb; but it also makes it clear that Gerald, being nursed by seventeen-year-old Dollie Armstrong after spraining his ankle, had no firsthand knowledge of the situation. Gerald emerges from his long introspection as from "a dark, narrow tunnel," with the pieces of his two puzzles fitted together, and feeling that he has been impeded for years by no more than "suspicions engendered by the words of a drunkard and the actions of a hysterical woman" (*ASA*, 183). At this stage, it seems enough to acknowledge to himself the possible truth of his suspicions, and that evening he writes to accept the editorship of the *History*.

In Book 2 action, too intricate to summarize adequately, largely replaces introspection, and in that the action is made to extend across almost the whole of a year, Wilson is able to give it unobtrusive reinforcement by relating it to the passage of the seasons. Chapter 1, starting in February 1955, shows Gerald acting with a renewed confidence, efficiently assembling contributors to the *History*, while at the same time working on his book on Edward the Confessor. To his professional confidence is added an emotional buoyancy that owes much to his romantic-sensual interest in Elvira Portway. This operates in two directions. While encouraging Elvira's and Robin's affair, not wishing them to repeat his own mistake of sacrificing love to "family," Gerald is also encouraged by Elvira to try to check his son John's homosexual liaison with the young, fey, unpleasant Irish boy, Larrie Rourke. (Inge has unwisely offered him accommodation in the hope of enticing John to visit her more often.) Gerald's impulse is well intentioned and laudable, a necessary part of his reeducation in human responsibility; but like all his belated meddling with his family (Wilson's name for him in the novel's manuscript was Gerald Medlicott), it fails utterly. With the Melpham problem, however, he is more successful. Reluctant to speak out, particularly because of the effect the revelation might have on the erratic mind of Rose Lorimer, Gerald is finally pushed into doing something by news of the Heligoland excavations: the pagan idol in Aldwin's tomb is likely to be interpreted in the light of Melpham, and thus lead to false historical generalizations, unless the "significance" of the Melpham idol (itself recently demonstrated to be genuine) is exploded.

Not only Iffley (who feels that Gerald's delay has been reprehensible), but Elvira and Kay indicate that Gerald's clear duty is to act, and chapter 2, set in summer, shows him seeking out what hard evidence of Gilbert's fraud may still remain, first from Lilian Portway, Elvira's grandmother, in Merano, then from Frank Rammage and Alice Cressett, the daughter of Portway's coachman Barker, who had been with Gilbert when the idol was "discovered." Each supplies a tiny hint to keep Gerald on what is now his crusade to restore "the good faith of a humane study in a world rapidly losing its humanity" (*ASA,* 286). As the pieces slowly assemble, Wilson gives violent examples of the inhumanity of the world to which history relates. Lilian Portway dies as a result of the drunken sadism of Stephanie Houdet's son Yves—an appalling French version of Larrie Rourke, who himself ends his stay at Inge's by stealing her jewelry and her car and driving her nearly hysterical by his revelations about John. The chapter culminates in an unholy mess of farce, bitterness, and near-tragedy: the literary party (Wilson's best bravura set piece in this novel) given by Robin's chillily conventional French wife Marie-Helene, the arid pretentiousness of which is rocked by the distraught arrivals of Elvira, whom Robin has parted from, and Larrie, who is on the run from the police; and the far-from-idyllic retreat of John and Larrie to a remote part of France, which ends in Larrie's death and the amputation of John's right leg.

The short, final chapter, which in terms of scale mirrors the novel's opening, takes place in autumn, appropriately a period for coming to terms. Gerald's final interview, with Harold Cressett, yields an important but inconclusive snatch of remembered conversation from Barker. Gerald is thus forced back to the person with whom his emotional life began and ended: Dollie Stokesay, whom he has not seen since the war and remembers as an alcoholic. Having resisted contacting her, he now feels a sense of release in knowing he must: he finds her living in the Cotswolds, a sprightly teetotaler and local magistrate, and reestablishes rapport with her immediately. He obtains from her not only a batch of Lionel Stokesay's papers, among them a conscience-stricken letter from Canon Portway which proves the truth irrefutably, but also a sense that his life as a man is not over. Dollie still doesn't want a permanent relationship—"you've got to move on," she tells Gerald later—but their friendship will certainly continue.

With his family, however, time has long since run out. Finding that Kay has quarreled with her husband and is living with her child at Inge's, Gerald goes to Marlow to persuade her to return to her husband Donald. Even that, he feels, would be better than re-becoming Inge's baby. Irritation with Inge provokes him to an accidental and splendid burst of anger—in contrast to his usual weary detachment—in the course of which he forces Inge to reveal what happened to Kay's hand: Inge had pushed her (accidentally) into the fire because

she was bothering John, then an infant and now a wheelchair conva-
lescent at Inge's. The revelation does not help Gerald, however:
whatever Inge did (and Kay has suspected as much), her daughter forgives her because it was she, and not her father, who brought the
children up. Gerald is rejected, leaving Inge both symbolically and
actually in control of "the pram and the wheelchair."

Since his family past is unredeemable, Gerald's professional redemption must be his only reward, though it is a real and large one.
It has its price, though: his disclosure, at an association meeting, of
the truth about Melpham quite unhinges Rose Lorimer, whose theo-
ries about the Celtic church have been based largely on the notion of
Eorpwald as a backslider. Calling Gerald a "damned traitor" and the
fraud story itself a concoction, she is consigned by a cruel authorial
irony to "an asylum near Whitby," at whose Synod the Celtic church
met its defeat by Rome. Offering, very properly, to resign the editorship of the *History* because of his delay in telling what he has half-
known for forty years, Gerald is supported by his colleagues, notably
and ironically by Clun, who admires John Middleton as a fighter for
truth and doesn't want to add to what he mistakes as Gerald's misery
over his accident. There is no irony, however, about Gerald's final
triumph, which in coming from Iffley is given a kind of imprimatur:
Gerald will become the next Chairman of the Medieval Association.

The end of the novel, a week before Christmas as at the beginning,
closes the circle of the year; but in flying to Mexico to see the Aztec
remains and work on his book, Gerald is shown as breaking free of
another circle, that of his own past. Wilson uses the same motif of a
plane journey to end *Anglo-Saxon Attitudes* as he did in *Hemlock and
After,* but now the hero himself is allowed to benefit from it. Instead
of death (for Bernard in *Hemlock and After*) there is self-forgiveness
and a future for Gerald. In terms of the "attitudes" of the novel's
title, Gerald, in vindicating Eorpwald, who now lies only physically,
has become fully upright himself.

Just before the novel's conclusion, Gerald dines with Robin and
Marie-Helene. At dinner he meets "Elizabeth Sands, the novelist's
daughter," whose mother has recently died. In 1957 Wilson ex-
plained his brief introduction of a character from his first novel into
his second thus: "it was self-indulgent to bring Elizabeth Sands into
Anglo-Saxon Attitudes: I felt that many people would like *Anglo-Saxon
Attitudes* better than *Hemlock and After*—and for the wrong reasons—
and I wanted to show them that the worlds of the two books were

the same."[10] In a sense, the worlds are the same: the academics who appear peripherally at Vardon Hall, and Bernard's sister Isobel, the professor of English, provide the central tableau of Wilson's second novel, and the moral problems created by Bernard's exacting humanism have their parallels—if not their equivalents—in Gerald's ultimate loyalty to the group-discipline of academe and the absolute values of honest history.

But there are certainly differences. Where Bernard seems vulnerable, Gerald is, if never complacent, then not exposed either to the full rigors of Bernard's self-criticism or to the disapproval of the public world. And whereas *Hemlock and After* conveys a feeling of fierceness and heterodoxy, *Anglo-Saxon Attitudes* has something of the satisfying richness of plum-cake, both because of the breadth of its social range and because the hero, as a heterosexual, is not set somewhat apart from the people among whom he moves.

Perhaps, in depicting a hero not only rich and admired when the novel begins but also successful when it ends, Wilson felt some twinge of self-reproach which cannot be apprehended by the actual reader of his novel. Certainly, despite being described by one reviewer as "long-winded,"[11] *Anglo-Saxon Attitudes* was also seen as treating its characters with more sympathy and affection than its predecessor; apart from Gerald, it contains some of Wilson's most sharply drawn and idiosyncratic characters, Inge, Dollie, and Elvira particularly. Most of all, it creates not only an intense involvement with story and character, but also the sense of its author's total competence in deploying a mass of incidents to make a complex fictional structure.

The Middle Age of Mrs. Eliot (1958)

Though about the same length as *Anglo-Saxon Attitudes,* Wilson's third novel, completed in July 1958, neither requires nor deserves the extended treatment given to its predecessor. The reason the novel does not require it is basically technical. Unlike those of *Anglo-Saxon Attitudes,* the multiple worlds that Wilson puts into this novel are not held together by complex interrelationships of time and character; they are juxtaposed to offer theoretically contrasted approaches to life, and are therefore susceptible of separate and more summary comment.

That *The Middle Age of Mrs. Eliot* should not deserve extended treatment may seem surprising since it won two literary prizes and drew from the *Daily Telegraph* a laudatory comparison between its heroine, described as "one of fiction's greatest heroines" and Gustave Flaubert's Emma Bovary. Nevertheless, Wilson's apparent choice here, of "taking you deep inside one person,"[12] is far from completely successful, since Meg Eliot and her predicament are not interesting enough to sustain a novel of this length. Indeed, Wilson's linking of her, early in the novel, with the heroines of novels by Jane Austen, George Eliot, Anthony Trollope, and Henry James is perhaps a subconscious admission of misgivings about her autonomous adequacy. Nor does the character with whom Meg is contrasted, her brother David Parker, have engaging enough human qualities to compensate for Meg's deficiencies. There is a remarkable difference between the uniform praise Wilson's third novel provoked in the better daily newspapers and the lukewarm response of the highbrow weeklies. The anonymous reviewer of the *Times Literary Supplement* called the novel "a brave and worthwhile failure"[13]; Goronwy Rees, in *the Listener,* spoke of its "uninspired competence from which life and vivacity seem to be missing," felt that its subject was unworthy of Wilson's abilities, and hinted that it would lose Wilson his original audience and gain him a larger, but less exacting one.[14]

The problem with the novel arises partly from its subject, and partly from the attitude that it exacts from its author. To sum up any novel in a single sentence is obviously to do it an injustice, but there is a sense in which it is fair to say that this one is about a middle-aged woman who loses her husband and becomes a secretary. The predicaments of Bernard Sands and Gerald Middleton, while capable of general application, are nevertheless not so common as to lose the characters their individuality: a good man who discovers in himself a disabling streak of sadism, a historian who has not faced up to a particular historical untruth. To lose one's spouse, however, and to adjust to the loss, is to be at once in a uniquely painful situation from the inside, and from the outside to be one of many. If the novelist emphasizes the affected character as someone different from others, he risks weakening the very predicament that creates the current of sympathy between reader and character; if he emphasizes the predicament, he risks reducing his character to a type. In deciding to have Meg lose her husband not, as first intended, by his suicide, but by a bizarre accident whose implications are hardly touched on, and by choosing to make Meg childless[15] and thus without those family responsibilities that would divert her personal grief, Wilson focuses his novel on the pure, existential element of Meg's position: what, now, is she, and how may she redefine herself?

With such a bedrock subject Wilson is not at his best; his difficulties are suggested if one compares *The Middle Age of Mrs. Eliot* with two other postwar novels, Francis King's *The Widow* (1957) and Doris Lessing's *The Summer Before the Dark* (1973). The heroine of the first, Christine Cornwell, is displayed coming to terms with the death of her husband against a historical backdrop some twenty years wide. Her practical struggles and her relationships with children and friends become, thus, part of an inevitable process of change and offer a moving, if not deeply original, illustration of human resilience. Indeed, the novel's strength lies in its exemplary ordinariness. By contrast, the experiences of Doris Lessing's Kate Brown, adjusting, not to the loss of a husband, but to the loss, in early middle age, of a clear sense of herself as a person, are presented with such directness and intensity as to raise a not-uncommon situation to the level of a unique vision.

Wilson's treatment of his subject, neither visionary nor simply poignant, is limited further by his very understandable wish to avoid details of satire or surface "realism" that might distract attention from the seriousness of Meg's position, exposed by widowhood and loss of wealth to a world she had not previously felt the need to understand. Reviewing *A Bit off the Map* in Autumn 1958, Martin Green pointed to the way in which Wilson's stories, and his second novel, constantly undermined a conscious moral intention with satirical depictions of the grotesque, a penchant of Wilson's judged by Green to reveal his real imaginative interest.[16] The texture of *The Middle Age of Mrs. Eliot* suggests an increased wish on Wilson's part to assert moral and metaphysical seriousness and to restrain those details of observation that might interfere with the reader's perception of it. It is significant that when conversing with Tom Pirie in Book 1 Meg notes "how awful it was for him not to be able to be intimate without spitting, and how impossible it was for her to register the one without the other."[17] In *The Wild Garden* Wilson pointed out that he "consciously identified" himself with Meg Eliot (*WGa*, 29–30), and one senses in this passage an authorial self-portrait amounting to self-criticism. Noteworthy also is the way that, confronted with the view of the desert on her journey to the Far East, neither Meg's reading of *The Mill on the Floss,* nor her sketching of an imaginary life for the stewardess Miss Vines, have power to shut out the annihilating blankness seen from the plane window. It was Wilson who saw that view first, six months before (*WGa*, 95), perhaps as a challenge to his fidgety, over-detailed interest in human variation. The result of these emerging new priorities, however, is that *The Middle Age of Mrs. Eliot* is a worthy novel that treats a serious theme seriously, but fails to illuminate it.

Wilson had first seen the desert in 1957, when flying to Tokyo to attend meetings of the P.E.N. Club. On the way he paused briefly at Bangkok, and it was there that "the seeds of the book were sowed" (*WGa*, 133). In the novel Bangkok is metamorphosed into the airport in the imaginary, hybrid town of Srem Panh, where Meg Eliot's barrister husband Bill tries to prevent the assassination of a local dignitary and is himself shot. What prompts Bill's action is never really made clear: reflex courage; admiration for the air of power emanated by the Badai minister, Prek Namh; an obscure quasi-suicidal impulse related to the money troubles and gambling debts he has left behind him in London? Its effect, however, is to leave his widow, at forty-three, with no insurance money, a house she does not own, and the need to cut the coat of her life to suit the drastically reduced cloth of her finances.

She has also, of course, to cope with her life's sudden emptiness without her husband, with whom, though unable to have children, she has had a happy sexual relationship, and to whom she has been content to leave most important practical decisions. At the same time, she feels guilty, realizing the reason for tensions evident in Bill at the start of the novel. After his death Meg comes to see them as, ultimately, the result of overwork in aid of their extravagant life-style in the Westminster area of London. Meg's natural wish to keep his memory alive, from which in the interests of her own life she gradually has to fight free, is intensified by her feeling that her too-unquestioning dependence on Bill has loaded him down.

It is, however, with Meg's loss of a husband and a life-style, rather than with any individuality of Bill's, that the novel is essentially concerned, dividing the two-year span of its narrative unevenly into three slablike books not broken into chapters: Meg "before" and Meg in two stages of "after." In its use of certain motifs Wilson's third novel repeats, combines, and extends its two predecessors. The start of Book 1, in which Meg is the unknowingly precarious elevated "Humpty Dumpty" of the title, recalls with its recurrent phrase "self-satisfaction" the opening of *Hemlock and After;* like Bernard,

Meg descends in Book 2 into chaos; but at the end of Book 3 she emerges, like Gerald Middleton, to a new life. The final uneventful plane journey to Hong Kong, as secretary to a labor delegation, is a happy echo of the plane journey near the novel's beginning, which is so absurdly truncated short of Meg's destination in Singapore.

Book 1 presents Meg's comfortable life as pregnant with what events reveal as ironies: her expression of loathing at the idea of being poor; her farewell party to which she invites, among others, her three "lame duck" friends, Lady Pirie, widow of a colonial governor, Poll Robson, a once-promising painter, Jill Stokes, widow of a naval officer; her amused sense of herself as a society hostess in the manner of Virginia Woolf's Mrs. Dalloway[18]; her attempts to soothe the "angry young man" resentments of Viola Pirie's son Tom (who when she is a widow makes a crude pass at her at someone else's party); her efficient handling of the charity cases brought before her at "Aid to the Elderly" and her pleasure in managing her colleagues on its committee. Her charm and ease, however, do not seem to constitute hubris, and the loss of her husband is not her tragic fate but the intrusion of chance, what Thomas Hardy calls "crass casualty." Whatever problems they cause her in Book 2, it is the social abilities and interest in people that Meg displays in Book 1 that are the source of her strength and that return her to a useful life at the end.

Premonitions of the emptiness to which Bill's death exposes her occur in Book 1, first in Meg's fear of the journey, something she calls "the horror in between" which only Bill's company can dispel; then in her mesmerized contemplation of the desert country of the Middle East, which leaves her "completely and absolutely bereft of all that made sense of her life, forsaken and ready for annihilation." Then, during her two weeks' convalescence in Srem Panh—perhaps the best section in the book, particularly in its convincing depiction of Meg's touchy relationship with the British Consular couple who are landed with looking after her—Meg's reduced status is given an oriental underlining when she tries with humanist conscientiousness to intervene in Badai justice. The intercession of a woman, and especially a widow, the Marriots tell her, will have no effect on the hanging of the disaffected young assassins, whose crime is not so much the killing of a British lawyer as the attempt to kill a Badai minister.

The exotic circumstances of Meg's crisis and the remoteness of Badai from her normal life give emphasis to her awareness of personal loss. Wilson succeeds in making her mixture of horror and trancelike calm moving to the reader in much the same way as a bereavement produces sympathy in real life: it is the more powerful for being displayed briefly. Meg's return to England to confront the problems of day-to-day living on a reduced scale, as metaphysically trivial as they are circumstantially protracted, can hardly be other than an anticlimax, and in Book 2's introduction of her brother David Parker, himself facing the imminent, and then the actual, death of his homosexual companion Gordon Paget, one senses a failure of nerve on Wilson's part, as well as his wish to provide Meg's search for an active modus vivendi with its opposite, a life-style based on passivity. In the shift of perspective in Book 3, which presents Meg not from the inside but as observed by David, there is an implicit admission that Meg no longer occupies the forefront of her creator's interest.

Wilson's method in Book 2, which covers the first three or four months after Bill's death, is simply to alternate the zigzag phases of Meg's "adjustment," which turns out to be premature and illusory, with descriptions of the more even tenor of life at Andredaswood,[19] the house in Sussex where David and Gordon have operated a commercial nursery garden, while also collaborating on botanical books and leading a life of disciplined quietism, Gordon's Quaker, David's agnostic-humanist. The punning and oddly skittish title of this longest section of the novel, 'Jobs for Job,' refers therefore not only to Meg, who enrolls on a secretarial course in order to equip herself for an independent life, but also to David, with his control of a staff of nearly forty people. Suffering loss they are Jobs, but so too is Gordon, dying of cancer, though his spirit, more buoyantly peaceful than David's, does not fear death. David, a former Oxford don, leads a life of "Martha daily duties and meditation": he feels that, in an age of violence, "we need a simmering down of human personality. . . . Otherwise all will be lost in the boiling over." (*MA*, 290). On his first appearance, his quietism is shown as taking the literal form of even "making as little noise as his very thorough morning ritual of washing and gargling allowed" (*MA*, 132).

The resultant atmosphere at Andredaswood is precious in a negative as well as a positive sense, as is evident in Wilson's recurrent, loaded use of the word "nursery." An ordered life will, in David's view, enable him to cross "the shapeless tract of human existence with grace and with gentleness" (*MA*, 201); but there is something childish, even a stale whiff of death-in-life, about the constant imposing of reason and restraint on the ordinary human irritations inseparable from any human endeavor, as is pointed up by the tensions among the chief gardener Tim Rattray, his deputy "Climbers" Lake, and the rose expert Collihole.[20]

Where David believes that "loneliness was the condition of man" (*MA*, 203), Meg's instincts are social. Though she refuses loans that would enable her to maintain some vestige of her former life, and instead sells her house and drifts away from her smarter friends, the isolation of hotels and bed-sitting rooms wears down her sense of identity, pushing her first outwards to acquire qualifications needed for a job, then backwards, as she visits or stays with the three old friends who, as widows and divorcées, "beckoned her to the circumstances to which she was now called"—a phase which, despite its bleakness, implies some possibility of renewal, and even expansion.

But the role models provided by Poll, Viola, and Jill prove unsuitable, even repellent, to Meg, however kindly intended by her three "Job's comforters." Poll's life of parties and borrowing, presented by Wilson with graphic depressingness, would be "to settle for being a slut," and Meg is not looking for "punch-drunk bliss or any other sort of plucky death in life." For Viola, a woman is incomplete without a man; but in feeling herself to have been a parasite even on Bill, Meg cannot bring herself to think remarriage, without love, other than immoral. Finally, Jill's obsession with the memory of her officer husband is seen by Meg as a "surrender to death," making it impossible for Jill to achieve any reasonable relationship with her daughter and hostile son-in-law. Meg discovers, too, that now she is a widow, her relations with her friends, easy when the center of her life was elsewhere, become ultimately impossible when there is undue proximity and she tries, for the best of reasons, to "help."

Eventually, overstrain from the successfully completed secretarial course, a quarrel with Jill, and delayed shock from Bill's death combine into a psychologically credible nervous breakdown. This serves Wilson's schematic purpose: from active competition in London Meg is transferred to passive convalescence in Sussex, looked after by her brother.

But though she finds comfort in Andredaswood it is not long before Meg's social responses begin to function. David's quiet regime, and his solicitude in driving her around the countryside, bring back her confidence; but it is more and more on Meg's own terms—charming people and managing affairs both domestic and professional (as temporary secretary first to a local headmaster, then to an ambitious member of Parliament)—that this confidence operates. Indeed, Meg's return to life is so assumed by Wilson that its later phases are seen not from Meg's point of view but from David's. That is, they are not so much experiences as phenomena, as though Wilson had lost interest in Meg herself and had become more concerned with her dynamic effect on the static personality of David.

The title of Book 3, "Nursery Ins and Outs," is again a pun, suggesting at once the disturbance created by Meg in the delicate network of relationships at Andredaswood, and also, more important, the way in which Meg and David change places during their reenactment of childhood affections and dependencies. Where at first Meg seems dependent on David, distracting him from his horticultural concerns, later he comes to depend on her, willingly absorbing himself in an eighteenth-century literature project at least as much for the sake of her companionship as for itself. In his notes for the novel Wilson originally contemplated having Meg take a lover. Instead, the sibling relationship fulfills this function: Meg sees herself as Jane Austen's Emma and David as Mr. Knightley, and Wilson coincides with the reader's growing sense of an incestuous closeness by having Meg say to David: "We don't want our life to get too cosily brother and sister. It wouldn't be quite decent" (MA, 393).

Perhaps it was some sense of skirting forbidden, if potentially interesting territory, that caused Wilson to move the novel quickly to the conclusion implicit in its static/dynamic dichotomy and in the relative unreflectingness of Meg. At any rate, Meg's final twelve weeks at Andredaswood move past like an accelerated film, covering only thirty pages to an ending hardly less perfunctory than it seems inevitable; though Meg's decision to leave, prompted by her guilty feeling that she is warping David's "real living peace" into mere "vegetable ease, creeping lethargy," produces one of the most moving exchanges in the novel, coming just after a shared evening that David, perhaps proving her right, judges to have been the happiest in his life. But the rapidity of the last two pages, in which news of Meg's various secretarial jobs over the next year reaches David by letter, conveys not only the feeling that Meg has passed beyond the ken of David—now over the worst of the loneliness caused by her departure—but also the feeling that Wilson has receded from both of his characters. One is almost left wondering what all the detailed fuss has been about.

Chapter Five

The Liberal at Armageddon

Having ended his first decade as a novelist with a book open to the charge of being dull and uneventful, Wilson entered his second with one that was, at first sight, so surprising and so different as to seem like an overcompensation. There is no doubt that *The Old Men at the Zoo* (1961) is a more exciting book than its predecessor, and John Wain, reviewing it in the *Observer,* went so far as to call it "for sheer energy and unexpectedness . . . the best of his books so far."[1] Other responses were not so unequivocal, and ten years later, in an interview, Wilson expressed his own affection for the book in slightly defensive terms: *"The Old Men at the Zoo* is perhaps loved by me very much because it has never—or has only recently—been much admired by the public."[2] At the same time, however, he inscribed in a copy of the novel in the library of the University of Iowa his view that it was his best book.

The Old Men at the Zoo is certainly a remarkable performance and in some ways unique in Wilson's work. It is his only novel to be set in "the future," though that future is already, for the present critic, ten years in the past, and did not involve Wilson in the radical re-imagining of human nature and society that George Orwell, writing in 1948, attempted in *1984.* It is Wilson's only novel to concern itself so fully with "the organization man." It is his only novel to be presented by a first-person narrator, who reveals his own limitations, as well as simply his own characteristics, in the course of describing the people he works with and the disturbing events in which he and they are caught up.

Nevertheless, though new and unexpected technically, Wilson's fourth novel can be more accurately viewed as a development and consolidation of themes that had preceded it. It develops the active/ passive dichotomy explored in *The Middle Age of Mrs. Eliot,* the more interestingly for placing this within a single character, the hero Simon Carter; and Carter's sense of responsibility to the zoo of which he is secretary is an outgrowth of Gerald Middleton's final loyalty, despite financial independence and the temptation to play down the importance of the Melpham hoax, to his fellow historians and their shared discipline. The conflict in Carter between his hankering to resume independent research as a field naturalist and his activities, alternately cramping and fulfilling, as an administrator, is prefigured also in a novel that Wilson began at the end of the 1950s but abandoned after fifty pages, entitled "Goat and Compasses." The components of the title—the name of a public house in an imaginary English cathedral city—stood in Wilson's mind respectively for two opposed elements in human nature: the irrational, described as "free and browsing where it will,"[3] and the orderly. The hero, Bill Greenacres, was evidently to be set the problem of harmonizing the two elements, something Carter does not fully succeed in doing. Carter's external difficulty, that of choosing a responsible moral course for himself while assisting the different projects of successive Zoo Directors, is anticipated in Wilson's description of Greenacres, in his notes, as someone who "has always avoided moral choices": Carter finally overcomes his tendency to temporize, to cooperate, to see the best in his superiors, just in time to regain credit as a committed human being.

Written in late 1960 and early 1961, *The Old Men at the Zoo* belongs to the same period as Wilson's Northcliffe Lectures, given in 1961 at the University of London. Entitled "Evil in the English Novel,"[4] they were much exercised by what Wilson saw as, by and large, the debilitating absence of evil from the English novel. With a few exceptions, including Samuel Richardson in *Clarissa,* Emily Brontë in *Wuthering Heights,* Joseph Conrad in *Heart of Darkness,* and E. M. Forster in *A Passage to India,* Wilson felt that English novelists had been too taken up with the domestic, the social, and the moral alternatives of right and wrong as opposed to the "transcendent values" of good and evil, their novels consequently having diminished vitality and a narrowed scope. In his first lecture Wilson spoke of having been "concerned to find ways of introducing evil into my novels," by which he implied a wish neither for Gothic horror nor for emotional sensationalism but rather for the expansion of the novel's capacity to express life fully.

Essentially, Wilson's use of the term "evil" seems to be a shorthand device, conveying a need to make the novel more powerful. His ways of introducing evil into his novels of the 1950s do not always succeed; the phrase itself suggests a suspiciously ersatz process. The treatment, in *Hemlock and After,* of Mrs. Curry and Hubert Rose, to

Bernard Sands alleged embodiments of evil, has a touch of the literary about it, suggesting nineteenth-century melodrama and decadence. Evil in *Anglo-Saxon Attitudes* is more pervasive and carries more conviction: the pagan nature of the Melpham idol, as well as Gilbert Stokesay's ritualist malice in "planting" it, the violence of Larry Rourke and Yves Houdet, the silent malignity of Alice Cressett. But, whether successful or not, these earlier manifestations all foreshadow Wilson's awareness, in *The Old Men at the Zoo* as in the contemporary Northcliffe Lectures, of life as something too large, too complex, too energetic, and too primeval to be contained within categories of right and wrong, however necessary and proper it is for human beings to attempt to contain and control it. *The Old Men at the Zoo* gradually reveals itself as a novel in which yet another liberal humanist—for Simon Carter is one, despite his concern for efficiency and his personal chilliness—is confronted by challenges to his position, challenges larger, more public, and more powerful than Wilson's first three novels had presented.

The biggest challenge to Carter's orderly and essentially humane view of life comes from the war, which devastates England in chapters 5 and 6, and allows the rise to the top, in chapter 7, of the Uni-European "scum" led by Blanchard-White, with his sinister ambition "to see justice done and to have a little fun." These events embody evil. Yet the novel offers another challenge, a much subtler and in part a humbling one, in being set almost throughout in the world of the zoo and the nature reserve: that is, in presenting a metaphor for man's encounters with the animal kingdom.

Wilson spoke in 1960, in his Ewing Lectures, of his long-standing love of "animal fables, animal stories, natural history books, above all zoos" (*WGA,* 77) and there is nothing accidental or incidental in his use of a zoo in this novel. To a certain extent its function is to supplant the images of gardens and gardening that figure in his work from "Fresh Air Fiend" to *The Middle Age of Mrs. Eliot:* the zoo is a kind of "wild garden," while the projected nature reserve is a kind of "garden in the wild." One can only applaud the replacement: despite widespread interest in gardening, gardens lack the power as a literary device that zoos, inhabited by animate creatures, possess, and Wilson's aesthetico-moral use of flowers and plants in his work is often too privately precise. His frequent references to animals in his earlier work are much more telling, since they "place" his characters in a way more accessible to the reader: the unseemly, patronizing tone used toward animals by Maurice Legge in "What Do Hippos Eat?"; Celia Craddock's threat to have her son's Muscovy ducks killed; Larry Rourke's apparent enjoyment when he puts the young owl out of its misery; Gilbert Stokesay sadistically showing Dollie pictures of tortured animals; Gordon Paget gassing his pets before he dies, which gives the reader an idea of the arrogant hardness of his particular Christianity; Meg Eliot's sensitive enjoyment of, and empathy with, the gibbon that swings about outside her window in Srem Panh. In *The Old Men at the Zoo* Wilson is able to ally these mostly moral discriminations with a sense of "transcendental values" insomuch as animals, while a human responsibility, are also a necessary reminder to man that orders of beings other than himself exist. Thus the novel's chosen frame of reference enables it to deal with a larger range of "human" relationships than most novelists have attempted.

Simon Carter, at thirty-five Wilson's first younger main character,[5] has some similarity to Wilson himself, as Wilson admitted was possible: "Simon's character may finally be a self-disguise: I don't know," he told Frederick McDowell in 1971. Not only does Simon's interest in animals echo Wilson's own, but also the "organization" framework of the novel derives much of its verisimilitude from Wilson's experiences at the British Museum, as a minor official and later as a Deputy Superintendent, and less congenially at Bletchley Park working for the Foreign Office during the war. At the same time, though, he has explicitly declared that it was easier to say "I" because Simon was not himself but based on a friend.[6] This simultaneous detachment and partial identification helps to explain the presentation of Simon as one who not only recounts events as he sees them, but realizes himself as they unfold. Wilson's notes indicate his intention clearly: "For Quentin [Simon's original name, finally used in *No Laughing Matter*] the novel must be a discovery of them [the "Old Men"] and through them of himself." Elsewhere, himself discovering part of the drift of his own book in his usual preliminary notebook process of "thinking aloud," Wilson suggested Simon's predicament as defined against the more single-minded but destructive obsessions of the "Old Men." It is a further restatement of the liberal dilemma that had haunted his work throughout the previous decade:

It would seem that what the book is saying is that insight (self and into others) is incompatible with activity and yet that activity's failures are too often the result of lack of insight.[7]

As administrative secretary to the London Zoo, Simon Carter is placed in a position that is never easy and sometimes impossible. When he has the chance to influence events, as when he prepares the zoo for a probable war by procuring 200,000 tons of sea water from the Bay of Biscay and storing it in blast-proof tanks,[8] and when, later, he orders the locking up of all zoo animals to protect them from a starving mob, he acts decisively and sensibly. Most of the time, however, he is responsible to a succession of directors, the "Old Men" of the title, all between sixty and seventy, whose pet schemes he must try to implement while neither completely agreeing with any of them nor being altogether clear about what overall policy he himself would pursue if Director, except for his own dream of a nature reserve devoted to indigenous British animals. Because he formerly worked at the Treasury, he is seen by some senior zoologists as a "sound man," and his support for Leacock's projected nature reserve for wild animals is influential, but he is suspect to some curators because he is "not a trained zoologist," and to junior research workers like Pattie Henderson he often seems to be "playing for the bosses."

Carter's position is further complicated by his own divided loyalties: on the one hand to administration, which he enjoys and feels useful in, on the other to his love of animals—he has been "the best naturalist on television"—and particularly of badger-watching which he tries to satisfy at a number of points in the novel, each time being deprived of a pastoral, innocent oneness with nature by complications of human behavior and political catastrophe. To his idealistic American wife Martha, on whose love he unduly depends for a refuge from "the terrible stress of public events,"[9] his true gift is as an observer of creatures and things. The passages in the novel (in chapters 3 and 4, and most important chapter 6) where he attempts to observe badgers are rendered with a lyrical delicacy unusual in Wilson's work. Yet despite what in chapter 1 Carter calls "all the incompetence and humbug that seemed inseparable from human beings,"[10] he nevertheless senses in himself "a natural liking for people," on both the personal and the official level, as "central to any meaningful life I could have" (*OMZ,* 52–53). At the conclusion of the novel, when it seems likely that Carter will become the zoo's director, he blames himself fiercely for undue "detachment" in the past and asserts his intention, sharpened by the recent chastening and frightening events, to be "more engaged with people and the animals."

The screams, animal and human, with which the novel opens, in May of "1970," serve like the supernatural in *Macbeth* and the pre-

ternatural in *Julius Caesar* to usher in the tensions and the power
struggles of the zoo, played out against "the many war scares of the
past years," and gradually subsumed within the darker, "Gotterdam-
merung" clouds of United Europe's attack on Britain. The death of
Filson, a young keeper of mammals kicked to death by, of all things,
a sick giraffe, poses for Carter a question of human responsibility, but
the zeal for justice with which he pursues this comes to seem abstract
and priggish: even Filson's father, Head Keeper of Birds, urges him
to drop the matter. The event, whose repercussions echo diminish-
ingly through the first two chapters, is used to introduce a spectrum
of zoo officials, including Langley-Beard, the Prosecutor, who ought to
have had the giraffe put down earlier, and Matthew Price, the admirable, officerlike eccentric Curator of Birds, who combines decent
human feeling with loyalty to the zoo's good name, but particularly
the zoo's Director, Edwin Leacock, and his deputy, Sir Robert Falcon, the most famous explorer and (with a futuristic touch) solver of
the mystery of the Himalayan yeti. Each wants a different future for
the zoo, Falcon favoring a return to the smaller zoo of Victorian times
which brought color and wonder to its patrons, Leacock with equal
passion lobbying for a large nature reserve in which wild animals can
enjoy "limited liberty."

Chapters 3 and 4, speeding up to cover the rest of 1970, describe
the rise and fall of Leacock's animal empire. The television program
narrated by Leacock, in which his dream of restoring a "lost countryside" to the "deadened soul" of urban man is vividly presented, deservedly provokes admiration from the normally cautious Carter, and
when the reserve is eventually opened at Stretton on the Welsh bor-
der, he escorts a trainload of animals transferred from London and
pays subsequent visits, feeling that "my life would really make sense
if I could settle down there." At the same time, he is squeezed between the needs of Leacock's rebellious and unhappy daughter Harriet, herself at "limited liberty" under her parents' supervision instead
of in prison for receiving stolen goods, and Leacock's appeals to him
to steer clear of her. Her angry arrival when he is silently watching
for badgers to appear both sexually humiliates him and scares the
badgers off.

A multiplicity of factors causes the reserve to fail. The concept
seems inherently unworkable: the animals cannot be protected from
their natural urge to escape, and when Leacock orders the shooting of
a recaptured lynx, his gesture, intended to restore public confidence,

backfires. Carter and other onlookers are sickened by a scene deliberately reminiscent of a ritual execution, and the reader feels only man's betrayal of the animal world. Politics also are involved. Lord Godmanchester, the zoo's president, but also a Churchillian statesman "in the wilderness," who desires office from a not-altogether-false belief that he alone can fend off war, has leased his Stretton estate only partly to help Leacock. His deeper motive is to encourage the sense that war is so imminent that even the zoo is evacuating, and thus to insure his recall to the government. When his plan succeeds, the continued existence of the reserve is an embarrassment. What finally closes it is the death there of Harriet, in circumstances so bizarre,[11] and with such potential for scandal, that Leacock, pressed by Godmanchester, feels obliged to abandon his experiment.

Despite pangs of loyalty to Leacock, Carter allows himself to be persuaded to stay at London Zoo under Falcon, who is mounting a neo-Victorian display (also reminiscent of the 1951 Festival of Britain) as the zoo's contribution to Godmanchester's "British Day," which is designed to restore public confidence at a tense time. As the political situation darkens, the splendid vitality of Falcon's devotion to his project comes to seem more like "fiddling while Rome burns," and when war breaks out, apparently as a direct result of Godmanchester's sudden death, Falcon's irresponsibility takes the form of switching on the "British Day" illuminations and setting off fireworks which depict patriotic and imperialist motifs. The scene has a mad, nostalgic grandeur: "we'll all go out as a high old, rare old, bloody beautiful joke" (*OMZ*, 276), Falcon declaims, before a huge explosion blows him up in the air to land, severely injured, on "the bronze lion that crowned the Lion House." In the bombing, however, the masses of wild animals placed by Falcon in the picturesque cages of the Old Victorian Zoo are burned alive—a Roman holiday that bitterly comments on Falcon's betrayal of his trust not only as director but even more as Curator of Mammals.

The remainder of the novel is a sequence of further climaxes, and events too involved to summarize justly. Britain is blockaded by European atomic submarines, and food shortages and the upset of public order lead first to the death of Matthew Price, bravely defending his precious parrots from a hungry mob, then to Carter's escape into rural Essex, driving a truckload of dead gorillas and live lemurs needed by the new director, Langley-Beard, for experiments that, at this stage, blend scientific single-mindedness with a crazed distortion of priorities. When the truck is stopped and the lemurs taken for food, Carter continues on foot on a nightmarish journey in which, ultimately, the sheer human need to survive triumphs over his devotion to animals. Watching, after so many abortive attempts earlier, the "happy family play" of four badgers—the size, significantly, of his own family—and soothed by their "healing innocence," he nevertheless, out of a different loyalty, guides some starving country people to kill two of them. The meat tastes "rich and delicious," but Carter is unable to cope physically with his betrayal: as he violently vomits, "everything became dark, became nothing."

The last two chapters bring Carter to a final crisis, this time of human and political conscience. Peace is restored, and the zoo's Director is now the ironically named Emile Englander, the efficient yet civilized European-minded Curator of Reptiles, whom Carter has previously admired. Under the new government, however—"Cultivated, rich, cautious, go-ahead old men who . . . substituted sense for sentiment and were about to substitute prosperity for patriotism" (*OMZ*, 312)—Carter's renewed work for the zoo looks more like collaboration, especially as Englander cannot restrain the Uni-European Movement which is being given its head. "European Day" at the Zoo, under the baleful influence of the "expectant alligator"[12] Blanchard-White, takes the ghastly form of police repression of patriotic hecklers, and the exhibition, and later killing, of a caged eagle and a chained bear, pathetically "representative" of America and Russia which at an earlier point had tried to restrain England and Europe from going to war. Too involved with zoo administration to realize fully what is going on around him, Carter is seen by Pattie Henderson as a time-server, and is left by his wife Martha, whose simpler integrity drives her into working for the Resistance. Eventually, after the arrest of Pattie and of Sanderson, a saintly, if sometimes foolish curator who, like Price, is an index of moral decency throughout the novel, and the unwillingness or inability of Englander to do anything, Carter faces up to his "untenable" position, plumbs Dostoevskian depths of remorse, and makes an inefficient attempt to intervene just as Blanchard-White is proposing to a horrified Englander that the zoo institute educative "spectacles": neo-Roman contests, exemplifying "the rich vein of Mediterranean brutality on which our European legacy so much depends" (*OMZ*, 317), between political prisoners and wild beasts.

The end of the novel is left open. By mechanisms that Wilson's use of a first-person, "future" narrator allows him to avoid fully describing, as the "future" reader, existing in Carter's world, can be presumed to know them, good government is restored on "Liberation Day," and Carter, whose six months in Enfield Camp have enabled him, just, to "work his passage in the Resistance," emerges as Acting Director of the zoo, with some chance of becoming Director and resuming a marriage much strained by previous events. The new world "excites" Carter "enormously," but his reason for the feeling is significant. Hales, the zoo's vice-president, is already rewriting the past, seeing the old era of "Leacock, Beard, Falcon, and that old swine Englander" as "a very bad period in the Zoo's history." For Carter, who has defended Englander at his trial, when he was wrongly under suspicion for abetting Blanchard-White's schemes, history is not so simple. Carter is excited by the new world "especially because I shall always be deeply involved with the old." A more benign version, perhaps, of Peter Lord in *The Mulberry Bush,* Carter seems intended by Wilson as someone who will combine the best traditions of liberal tolerance with the ability to act clearly when that is the right thing to do. Carter's final reference, however, to the giraffe with which the novel began suggests the unpredictability of the world, both animal and human, in which he must operate.

There is no doubt that *The Old Men at the Zoo* is a most impressive novel. It has some of the fierceness of *Hemlock and After,* but combines this with a larger thematic and symbolic range than any other of Wilson's novels. As well as showing the civilized indispensability of liberalism, it suggests its weaknesses: in Carter, a frivolity used to avoid difficult confrontations, and a habit of caution not always to be distinguished from physical cowardice. The range of attitudes to animals is very fully demonstrated: the devoted, the cruel, the protective (shading into the sentimental), and the scientifically objective (shading into the exploitative). What poignantly emerges, in the encounters between Simon and badgers, and in the eerie scene (chap. 4) in which out of a mixture of fears he shoots Harriet Leacock's dog, is the near-impossibility for man of achieving a harmonious and innocent relationship with the animal world.

If one considers *The Old Men at the Zoo* as a novel of the future, its handling of political affairs is sometimes arbitrary and vague, partly as a natural result of the use of a first-person narrator. Despite having received, in the novel's planning stages, a helpful scenario entitled "The War of 1971" from the eminent military historian Michael

Howard,[13] Wilson does not manage to make it quite clear why things happen as they do. But the affinity of *The Old Men at the Zoo* is not with such novels of the future as Orwell's *1984* (1949) or L. P. Hartley's *Facial Justice* (1960), both of whose social worlds are some degrees removed from immediate recognition. A better parallel is C. S. Lewis's *That Hideous Strength* (1945), though Wilson's book is a novel not a fable, and agnostically dispenses with Lewis's Christian-supernatural machinery. Both have in common the motifs of an organization that takes on nightmarish and evil proportions and a hero who only at a late stage recognizes the need to break free from it.

The root of the matter is that *The Old Men at the Zoo* is not, despite trivia like Princess Anne's visit to the South Pole mentioned in chapter 1, a novel of the future, but a novel of the past, and an extremely powerful one. As its political situation worsens, one feels not a sense of incredulity nor, simply, of approaching doom but a flesh-creeping sense of déjà vu. Vichy is mentioned, as is the ominous phrase "peace with honor." In the disbelief of Carter and Englander in the real intentions of the Uni-Europeans one recognizes 1930s appeasement, and Blanchard-White's followers behave like Hitler's National Socialists or Sir Oswald Mosley's Blackshirts. The very term "old men" recalls the politicians with whom Edward VIII was impatient,[14] and the "men of Munich" with whom Lionel Stokesay aligned himself.

Wilson's original intention had been, in fact, to set his novel "in a triumphant German invasion of England in 1940";[15] but the possibility of libel suits from real London Zoo officials of that period caused him to change his mind. One critic at least discerned this intention through the lineaments of the published novel. This was Evelyn Waugh, who considered it "a very fine book" with characters "brilliantly observed and drawn." In a long letter to the *Spectator* in 1961 he placed its events in their historical perspective:

If I read him right, [Wilson] is concerned with what might have happened, rather than what will happen. Consciously or unconsciously he has written a study of 1938–1942. . . . He required a war for his plot and the war he has given us is what many Englishmen feared at the time of Munich. . . . Communications would cease. Famine would ensue. We should capitulate and the victors would impose a Nazi regime. The young may find it hard to believe, but that was in fact the belief of many intelligent people.[16]

Wilson was not imagining a future, but remembering and exorcising the past, and the novel's force largely derives from its extension into history of themes he had previously treated in entirely fictional terms. But to Waugh's comments one may add another. What did not happen in 1940 in England did happen in Nazi-occupied Europe, so that for critics to object on the grounds of verisimilitude, as some did, to the intended excesses of Blanchard-White is beside the point. The haze of insufficient political detail in *The Old Men at the Zoo* reveals behind itself a true and looming horror.

Chapter Six
Past and Present

In *The Old Men at the Zoo* the emotional atmosphere, though not the exact factual truth, of the comparatively recent past is translated into the not-too-distant future. Wilson's two other novels of the 1960s delve back without disguise into the more remote historical past contemporary with his own birth in 1913, and move forward from this into the actual present of their writing. *Anglo-Saxon Attitudes* had done something like this in returning to 1912; but its long sequence of flashbacks is presented in a reverse order appropriate to the novel's character as a psychological, as well as a historical, detective story: time is seen as an ever-present continuum in Gerald Middleton's mind, offering him the opportunity to reappraise himself. With *Late Call* (1964) and *No Laughing Matter* (1967), which both begin in the past, the sheer span of years between past and present contributes an element of built-in pathos: in *Late Call* a blank hole of fifty years spent, the reader is left to infer, on matters of no real significance; in *No Laughing Matter* the more orthodox panorama of inevitable change through six decades. In these two novels one experiences time as having physical weight and thickness, independent of the people who inhabit it; and one has the feeling that Wilson, in the second of his three decades (so far) as a novelist, was compelled to embrace and master in fiction the whole century through which he had lived, before he could return in the early 1970s to the immediately contemporary.

Late Call (1964)

Two aspects of Wilson's discarded novel "Goat and Compasses" came to fruition in *Late Call* five or six years afterwards. One was housing estates; the other was the structural notion of a novel divided into a prologue and a main story set some years later.

The main story of "Goat and Compasses" begins with the official opening in 1957 of a complex of workers' housing called the Hargreave Estate; that of *Late Call* is set in the imaginary "New Town" of Carshall somewhere on the southern edge of the Midlands, a location whose atmosphere in part recalls Wilson's short stories "A Flat Country Christmas" and "Christmas Day in the Workhouse." The emotional force of the latter story in particular is related to the nervous breakdown that Wilson suffered while working in the Midlands, at Bletchley Park, during the war, and it is possible that the isolation and alienation experienced, and overcome, by Sylvia Calvert at Carshall represents Wilson's final sublimation, twenty years later, of that unhappy period in his life.

The "New Towns"—initially Stevenage, Crawley, Hemel Hempstead, and Harlow, all within thirty miles of London—had been established in 1946 by the recently elected Labour Government, partly to rehouse Londoners made homeless by the wartime bombing, partly to provide relocated industrial enterprises with a work force, and partly as an experiment in social engineering. With their functional new architecture, their modern art, and their attempt to loosen the stratified British class system, they were seen by their supporters as the vanguard of a "brave new world"; to their detractors they seemed disruptive of the countryside, rootless and soulless. The final phase in the expansion of Stevenage, in late 1960, had aroused controversy locally and in the national press; this, and the fact that in 1961 fifteen more New Towns were in process of construction, may have prompted Wilson, socialist by politics but far from narrowly doctrinaire, to wish to look at the New Town phenomenon and assess how well it had worked out in human terms. Certainly his wish for factual authenticity is suggested by the large amount of information about New Towns contained in his notes for *Late Call,* which is, indeed, the only novel with such a setting by an important British writer.

Wilson's decision to look at a little-known area of postwar British life deserves respect, though Stephen Wall in a review described the novel as "worthily pedestrian,"[1] and it is not difficult to imagine readers for whom the insular preoccupations of Carshall seem as dreary as the quietist niceties of Andredaswood. "It seems to be much down on my usual social scale," Wilson accurately—and perhaps worriedly—forecast in his notes, and when his conscientious concern for local color drives him, in chapter 7, to mention local ten-pin bowling teams embarrassingly named "the Mellingerers" and "the Bowling Budgies," one is unsure whether such unknown territory deserved his interest. In his lectures on "Evil in the English Novel" he had already indicated that "felt sociology" was a very limited aim, pursued by too many British novels, and that is all *Late Call* would be, if it were no more than a depiction of a New Town on its own terms.

The novel is considerably more than this, however, and the "more" is created by its human point of view, that of 64-year-old Sylvia Calvert, who like Wilson himself is the product of an earlier age and thus able to function as an "innocent eye" through which Carshall and the modern world it represents can be observed. What is more important, the novel is her story. Unusually for a Wilson novel employing the third-person method, everything (apart from the Prologue) is seen from her single viewpoint: it is the tension between her past and her present that provides the novel's energy, and her late self-realization is its essential subject. Her name, Sylvia, is not a random choice: not only does it suggest "sylvan," appropriate to her rural origins, it also suggests the song beginning "Who is Sylvia?," which in Victorian fashion could be *Late Call's* subtitle. The course of the novel is to demonstrate that the answer is not "our granny," as on her son Harold's rhyming Christmas card in chapter 2; she is an individual, though it has taken her the whole of her life to make this discovery.

Any novel of merit persuades one to a second reading, but *Late Call* is so constructed that it needs this in order to be fully understood. The Prologue, accurately set in "The Hot Summer of 1911,"[2] has been described by nearly all commentators as a short story in itself. In that it begins and ends with the viewpoint of Mrs. Longmore, a fashionably dressed Chelsea lady of aesthetic, liberated outlook who has brought her two children for a holiday on a Suffolk farm, it has the necessary air of self-containment, and in demonstrating to the reader and to Mrs. Longmore herself the limitations of her privileged attitude it is an excellent picture, satirical yet poignant, of the hostilities underlying the pre-Great War class system, of the clash between half-baked "progressive" ideas and childhood innocence, and of the gulf between the city's idyllic vision of rural life and the real thing. The Prologue's connection with the body of the novel, however, does not essentially reside in Mrs. Longmore (mentioned only once later, in passing), but in the ten-year-old eldest daughter of the Tuffields, the family at the farm.

Nameless throughout, the Tuffield girl provides the more haltingly articulate point of view of the Prologue's central section. Tempted by seven-year-old Myra Longmore away from the "sad, listless and neglected" brood of siblings it is her job to look after, she spends some hours wandering through meadow, brook, and wood, enjoying a unique glimpse of childhood and "doing something different"—as she feels Mrs. Longmore would approvingly put it. In the course of a kind of symbolic journey into Eden she progressively removes her layers of hot clothing and urges Myra to do the same:

> She was content, lying back in the warmth of the leaf-dappled sunshine, just to be; she could not remember such a thing before, she could only recall doing things or thinking about things to be done.[3]

But with a subtle touch of directional irony, the path away from dreariness and premature responsibility bends back by the edge of the rectory garden to nearly its point of origin. Disheveled, the two children become a spectacle for sniggering, prurient neighbors, and Myra blames the Tuffield girl, who ends up getting slapped by her mother and sadistically "bum-basted" by her father. "Play" is all right for the gentry, but hers is a life of "work": though she may seem "special" and "possessed of a sense of beauty and wonder" to Mrs. Longmore—who nevertheless has a strong streak of prudery and snobbery under her "modern" ideas—to her mother, grimly aware of lower-class social realities, the girl is "Nothin'. And you always will be."

The transition from the rural Prologue to the first chapter, in which Sylvia Calvert is retiring from her job managing a seaside hotel on account of high blood pressure, is disorienting to the first-time reader of *Late Call* and is intended to be: "how to disguise Sylvia in Chapter I?" is a question that figures in Wilson's notes for the novel. To quote his question makes it clear that a connection, established at different speeds by different readers, does exist between the Prologue and the rest of the book.[4] Sylvia Calvert is, in fact, the eldest Tuffield girl fifty years on, and the reason for Wilson's wishing to obscure the link for the reader is because it is only after some months at Carshall that she herself perceives it: while gradually picking up clues to Sylvia's identity, the reader is meant to share with her a more important experience—the recovery of a long-buried awareness of the past, and the bridging of the gap between present and past whose width is in the first instance unrealized because of the quick leap (one page to the next) from Prologue to first chapter. For all its limitation of social and intellectual scale after its predecessors, *Late Call* is technically innovative: it questions the novel's very conventions of selection, which implicitly suggest that what lies undescribed between chapters does not exist.

Various indications in chapter 1 suggest that, without herself knowing it, Sylvia has learned the harsh lessons of her childhood only too well. She distrusts the "personal note," feeling that, throughout her life as a hotel manageress, "she'd never done more than her duty"; thus she lacks the "self-worth" to enjoy the praise bestowed on her by residents of the Palmeira Court on her retirement. "Keep your feelings for your own flesh and blood" is her motto, a sadly limiting one in that two of her three children have died quite young. In non-professional relationships with strangers—such as an American couple met on the train to Carshall—she is wary and embarrassed, unlike her irrepressible older husband Arthur, a "raffish old sport" type consciously based on Wilson's father, who strikes up acquaintance easily, if touchily, and enjoys embroidering his past as an acting-Major in World War I. Reading in the "Eastsea" paper an item on their departure from the town after fifteen years, Arthur is angry that their name is misspelled "Culver"; Sylvia, very much her mother's daughter, merely comments "We're not important people." The point is driven home by Wilson more crudely when Sylvia is "settling in" (chapter 3) at Carshall; confronted by her son Harold and the hearty welfare officer Sally Bulmer with a questionnaire that asks her "What are you?," she answers: "I'm a nobody. I always have been."

For Wilson, however, as for Arthur Miller in *Death of a Salesman,* "attention must be paid to such a person,"[5] and he manages to give her slow journey from winter to summer, from nobody to somebody, not only a touching interest but even a subdued air of excitement. Having taken her leave (in the punningly titled first chapter) of a life of work, in favor of the leisurely "late call" symbolized by her presentation electric clock, Sylvia finds it hard to bear the "empty uselessness" of life in the chillily jovial, regulated household of her widowed son Harold, a school headmaster devoted to the memory of his courageous but hard-sounding wife and to "the New Town and what it stands for." Harold, whose tragic potential is undercut by his lower-middle-class pompositries of speech, combines good works and a frustrated devotion to Carshall's amenities with total lack of personal charm; an expert in remedial education, he is quite unable to understand his own children, one homosexual and all chafing against Carshall's small-world restrictions.

Though at the end of the novel Sylvia is able to assure Harold that he is "right to be proud of Carshall," and to bring him some comfort in his family troubles and the defeat of his passionate efforts to save Goodchild's Meadow from urban development, this is only because she herself has by then emerged from a dark tunnel of alienation. Her ability to accept her new world comes, rather like Simon Carter's, because she is at last aware of her roots in the old one, which for most of her life have been buried in her subconscious. To her, initially, the plastic, glass, and steel of Carshall make a world of "trees without leaves" in which she cannot feel at home; it is wryly summed up in her view of a modernistic fountain in the Town Centre: "it was clever but you couldn't say that it played" (chap. 4). At an amateur performance, organized by Harold, of John Osborne's *Look Back in Anger* Sylvia feels menaced by what seems to her the play's intolerance of old people, and she experiences "a muffling fog of horror" that she relates to postwar newsreels of Jewesses herded to the gas chambers; later, as she reads accounts of famous murders, this feeling reappears as an identification with the victims, old women "humiliatingly pulped into nullity" (chap. 6). Aware only of fear and claustrophobia, she retreats to the "shut-in safety" of television serials and romantic novels. Freedom from her old, busy life of mechanical "doing" leaves her a prey to the blankness of nonidentity, and on Good Friday her depression reaches near-suicidal proportions.

Sylvia's salvation begins on Easter Sunday, when at Carshall's modernistic church she hears an out-of-keeping sermon given by an ancient visiting clergyman, a Scot suggestively called Mr. Carpenter. His Calvinistic beliefs, not in hell fire but in the superiority of Divine Grace to human works, are "barbarous" and "rubbish" to Harold, but to Sylvia, old like the clergyman and with "no ties with this dressed-up, united congregation of Carshallites," they make an instinctive appeal, offering a route through "the dreadful silence . . . the dark nothingness" into light. The sermon, in fact, is the "late call" to true "being" to which the novel's title refers,[6] and Sylvia's light, though it is secular rather than religious, begins to dawn when she escapes from the lanes close to Carshall (which have a habit of bending back on themselves) and starts to explore the countryside (chap. 6), where her "new leaves" are to be found. Since her arrival in Carshall, the countryside has inspired in Sylvia's consciousness a pregnant mixture of dread and fascination; in chapter 5, for instance, she is made to wonder: "what is an old woman doing staring at the spraying of fields, and still more, gazing into the empty distance?" Eventually, in an image retrieved from memories of her daughter Iris, knocked down at fourteen by a lorry, Sylvia realizes the answer. The reknitting of the lost pattern of her life, like an unraveled jumper, is somehow to be accomplished by going "into the distance" surrounding her.

Sylvia's melancholy "wanderings abroad," along with offering places like the Rectory School which produce "a strange gale of memories" of her early life as a housemaid, bring her two important meetings. The first, essentially negative, is with a hunchbacked Polish woman in her seventies, whose life of vicissitudes in all the sensitive areas of twentieth-century political geography, from Europe to South Africa, is the "important" opposite of Sylvia's years in English hotels. Laced with made-up quotations[7] from classic European authors, the narrative is inset into chapter 6 under the title "The Old Woman's Story"; intended to create for the reader an "alienation effect," it is for Sylvia a vignette of rootlessness that leaves her "torn and sad," feeling sorry for someone worse off than herself, who seems condemned to go through a darkness without end or meaning.

Her other meeting, significantly in a May of unusual warmth, is with Mandy Egan, an American child whom she finds clinging in terror in a thunderstorm to an isolated tree which soon after is struck by lightning. The scene is tense with implicit symbolism—Sylvia's own fears of lightning, her practical instinct to rescue the child, the "funeral smoke" of the blasted "rotten oak"—and its aftermath operates as a kind of release mechanism for Sylvia's psyche. At the Egans' farm, with adoring child and grateful parents, Sylvia finds herself recalling her own farm childhood and the day described in the Prologue. Telling it all to Mandy, she sees her past as "happy summer country days," while also realizing how "it was bad to be poor" and coming to terms with her parents' harshness.

Throughout chapter 7, her "wonderful summer" with her new friends the Egans, she develops the self-confidence (manifested in a number of small ways) to cope with Carshall. In the final chapter, entitled "Harvest," she is able to bring some comfort to Harold and also to face the death of her husband and, with it, some forty years of her life. When Arthur dies of a stroke, she "lets go" her feelings in a passage that movingly conveys her sense of waste:

a desperate grief closed in on her, grief for all the years and years that had been nothing or worse than nothing, for tenderness dried up and tenderness drained away into indifference. (*LC,* 307)

But in speaking of Arthur to Harold after the funeral, she combines a loyal, spirited defense of his unsettled life—betting, borrowing, living from day to day, a gassed veteran unable to adjust to not being a wartime "temporary gentleman"—with awareness of the failure of a marriage led socially "on different floors" and with different expectations. It is, one feels, the recapture and consequent assessment of her earliest years that both enables her to admit the essential meaninglessness of her middle ones and to face with resilience a future in which, still in Carshall but in a flat of her own, she will at last function as an independent individual, as she did one day as a girl in 1911.

Despite the prosaic restrictedness of its New Town setting, whose details of character and story are nevertheless very sharply observed, *Late Call* is an emotionally absorbing novel, for two main reasons. One is the quality of poetry—unusual in Wilson—that the writing possesses when dealing with Sylvia's awareness first of psychological nothingness, then of the mysteriousness of the countryside; though its concern is with secular rather than religious "grace," the novel suggests the importance in human life of forces that another novelist might call divine. The second reason is the novel's structure, which embodies the notion of a memory forceful enough to rise to the surface years later and satisfyingly bring together the jagged ends of experience.

The difference between Harold's world of "doing" and Sylvia's regained sense of "being" is subtly suggested by the wording of the novel's conclusion. Playing at "bears and squirrels" with their questionnaire, Harold and Sally Bulmer are "new people" who inhabit the postwar culture crystallized by *Look Back in Anger* (1956), from which the phrase is taken. Sylvia, however, does not look back in anger, but with the understanding that forgives and therefore benefits. The phrase Harold uses to describe her—"You're in good form these days, Mother"—curiously resembles the last phrase of Evelyn Waugh's *Brideshead Revisited* (1945), in which the past survives with power for the present. And in the overall structural sense it gives of the past's ability, when faced up to and re-envisioned, to offer hope for the future, *Late Call,* though operating on a lower social level, has distinct affinities with another novel concerned with a hot, distant, traumatic summer, L. P. Hartley's evocative *The Go-Between* (1953).

No Laughing Matter (1967)

Wilson's sixth and longest novel (its central section alone is as long as *Late Call*) is both innovative and old-fashioned. The old-fashionedness lies in its ambitious grasp at the panoramic: six decades of changing England, from the misty, hopeful, still imperial days "Before the War" to the less heady, post-Suez world of "emergent nations." This historical process is embodied through the lives of three generations of the upper-middle-class Matthews family, and especially in the variegated experiences of the six Matthews children, born between 1897 and 1904. In generic terms, *No Laughing Matter* is a family saga, an attempt by a postwar novelist to recapitulate and preserve the texture of a past coextensive with his own, to mine and transform a rich vein of personal family memories, and in so doing extend the vitality of a form synonymous in British literature with John Galsworthy in *The Forsyte Saga,* but adopted also by Arnold Bennett in *The Old Wives' Tale* and the *Clayhanger* sequence,[8] and by Virginia Woolf in *The Years,* which like Wilson's novel uses chosen years as section-divisions.

One's sense of the novel's old-fashioned, traditional nature is cumulative, the effect to a large extent of its verbal and situational density, and of the sheer amount of historical time that has been got through by the end: the dry, local irony of the final phrases offsets, but does not cancel, a satisfying balance of triumph and sadness at lives lived and lives almost over. What more immediately catches the eye, however, during the course of reading is Wilson's technical virtuosity, the range of his methods of presentation.

Not all of these can strictly be described as innovative. Book 2, the longest depiction of a single year (1919), is a sort of mini-*Ulysses* in choosing to concentrate on just a twenty-four hour period, and that part concerned with the small hours of Sunday morning at the Matthews family home in the Westminster/Victoria section of London is particularly reminiscent of James Joyce in the earthy way in which it successively exposes the consciousnesses of members of the family, as well as that of their cockney cook Henrietta Stoker, known as "Regan." Here, for instance, is Gladys, thinking of her father, William Matthews, who has come home drunk at half past midnight:

So that for you, Billy Pop, billygoat of fathers, bleating and ruttish, women don't all have to be your little grateful Gladeyes, nor like HER turned tigress by your failure, a mock tigress to be mocked.[9]

Elsewhere, one often thinks of Virginia Woolf, against whom Wilson in the 1950s had been in conscious reaction, objecting to her lack of interest as a novelist in the workings of the "moral will" and to her concomitant preference for showing her characters as immersed in the pleasures and agonies of simply existing.[10] A decade later this critical view had altered, and the alteration may be related to the gradual shift, in his own work from *Hemlock and After* to *Late Call,* in the emphasis given to "doing" as opposed to "being." In 1971 Wilson spoke admiringly of Woolf, not only pronouncing *The Waves* (1931) "a very great novel indeed," but admitting that "I had to fight very hard not to allow the scheme and so on of *The Waves* to obtrude in *No Laughing Matter,* where I was in fact dealing with six principal characters much in the same way as she did in *The Waves.*"[11] This awareness of Virginia Woolf is found in Wilson's notes for the novel, and though his choice of six for the number of the Matthews siblings may have its roots in his own life (Wilson had five brothers), his equal division of them between the sexes echoes her, as in part does his decision to make one of them, Margaret Matthews, a novelist like Virginia Woolf's Bernard. Only once does Wilson directly copy the first-person utterances of *The Waves,* in a short sequence toward the end of the playlet "The Russian Vine" (Book 3, section 2). Flanked by similar remarks by Gladys and Margaret, Sukey Matthews says: "I shall stand in the squalid kitchen clearing my little space for fresh vegetables and greaseless meat and I shall dream of manor houses and ordered voices and little creatures properly cared for" (*NLM,* 277). He clearly means the reader to recognize the allusion; but his frequent authorial immersion in his six characters' minds as they respond to sights and events represents an equal though less obvious use of Woolf's techniques.

For Wilson to enter his characters' thoughts and feelings in a manner reminiscent of Joyce and Virginia Woolf is stylistically appropriate in a novel the bulk of which is set in the interwar years when their work dominated the literary scene. The sharpening sociopoliti-

cal atmosphere of those years, rendered in Wilson's novel through the
activities of the disillusioned ex-officer and left-wing journalist Quentin Matthews and (to show how pervasive it was) even in the responses of his aesthetic, homosexual younger brother Marcus,
provides a link with another contemporaneous writer with whose
work Wilson had grown up in the 1920s and 1930s: Aldous Huxley,
particularly the Huxley of *Eyeless in Gaza* (1936). Thus the style and
the content of much of *No Laughing Matter* present Wilson as a self-
conscious writer, aware of both the historical "reality" of his material
and of the way that reality had been reflected in the work of novelists
older than himself.

This kind of authorial artifice, however, is not obtrusive and may
indeed not be noticed by many readers, who may simply feel that
they are sharing the lives of characters tied to history by well-known
events and the names of famous people (the later acting career of Rupert Matthews is defined in terms of these, as are Marcus's activities
in the world of art). Where the innovativeness of *No Laughing Matter*
really lies is in those sections that break the "realistic" conventions of
the novel and insist on its "fictionality." Wilson had already attempted something like this in 1953, in his "Scrap-Book of the
Twenties," *For Whom the Cloche Tolls.* This is not merely a piece of
fascinated nostalgia. The "period" lives of the fun-loving Maisie and
her children Bridget and Tata are distanced by means of a prismatic
method of storytelling, which employs extracts from various people's
diaries and letters and at the end presents Maisie as a marginal figure
in invented passages by writers of the period, including Huxley and
Virginia Woolf.

In *No Laughing Matter* Wilson from time to time interrupts the
absorbing effects of his narrative not only by ironically distancing authorial remarks (like the bracketed alternative descriptions of the
Matthews siblings at the start of Book 4), but by sections cast in dramatic form, beginning with the three-act "Family Sunday Play" in
Book 2, which shows the Matthews parents, "Billy Pop" and "the
Countess," at the height of their selfish, hypocritical, exuberant powers, and concluding at the end of Book 3 with "Pop and Motor: A
Catastrophe," in which their histrionic medley of recriminations, sentimental togetherness, and pathetic unfulfillment is finally shattered
by a German bomb. These various playlets, pastiches successively of
vaudeville turns (complete with asides to the "audience"), Shaw
("Parents at Play"), British imitations of Chekhovian gloom ("The

Russian Vine"), Terence Rattigan ("French Windows"), and finally, with a kind of anachronistic vengefulness, Samuel Beckett's *Endgame*, suggest the many ways in which "reality" has been apprehended in twentieth-century literature. They also give Wilson the opportunity, by means of elaborately cool stage directions, to show the changing physical appearance of his characters over the years and present them as quasi-historical "specimens" as well as individuals whose feelings demand and deserve the reader's empathy.

"Such alienating devices," Wilson said in 1971, "seemed to me peculiarly necessary in a bourgeois family saga novel where the reader is by custom likely to immerse himself and lose sense of the full meaning of the book."[12] Whether Wilson's devices alienate the reader in any important sense is debatable, since the overwhelming mass of the novel is forward-moving narrative with all the accustomed power-to-involve that narrative possesses. But the dramatic interludes do have the effect of making *No Laughing Matter* not only a review but a revue, and it is easy to agree with two other reasons Wilson gave for his variations of technique: the playlets exist "because the family is a self-dramatizing one," and are "partly . . . a way of lightening what is a very long novel."[13] There is no doubt that they contribute enormously to its vitality.

Balancing his wish to vary the texture of his "family saga" is Wilson's desire to unify it structurally by means of a theme. This theme is hinted at by the title, though in a way that runs the risk of making the former a mere truism: who would imagine that life in the twentieth century was a "laughing matter"? Life has not been this for Sylvia Calvert; no more, this novel makes clear, is it for the Matthews siblings, though they are all successful in their undertakings, even the imprisoned Gladys, who in refusing to think herself a victim of her lover Alfred's sly business dealings emerges bloody but unbowed. The true relevance of the "laughter" notion is made clearer in Wilson's early notes for the novel, held in the University of Iowa library: "the basic theme is mode and manners of defensive humour upon varying characters within a limited group."

The Matthews children, seen in Book 1 looking into the "laughing [that is, distorting] mirrors"[14] at the Earl's Court Exhibition of 1912, are all prone to various types of humor—Gladys's clownish, Marcus's malicious, Margaret's ironic, Quentin's bitter, Sukey's whimsical, Rupert's sentimental and stagy. Throughout the novel—punctuated in leitmotiv fashion by words like "comedy" and "laughter"—these forms of humor are exposed and evaluated, either tacitly, by contrast with the circumstances in which they occur, or overtly, as with Margaret's comments on her restrictive habit of irony in her fiction, and in the Matthews children's occasional direct expression of impatience with the efficacy of "The Game," the ritual they devise in order to assert themselves by mimicking their parents. First occurring between Rupert and Marcus as a defense mechanism against the Countess's hostility to the latter ("black monkey," "dirty little wetabed"), "The Game" emerges full-blown at the end of Book 2 when the five younger children act out their parents before the eldest, Quentin, who as "Mr. Justice Scales" pronounces sentence on them as individuals (for perfidiously drowning the kittens that Sukey has tried to mother), and as representatives of a shabby-genteel, hypocritical, dying "system and class" that has no place in the modern world.

The final, brief occurrence of "The Game" comes in 1946, when the six "children" revisit their former home to sort out their dead parents' effects. By this time they have carved out their own careers and fulfilled many of the dreams expressed in their responses to the Wild West Show with which the novel begins, that one short interlude of "happy carefree intimacy" which the whole family "had scarcely known before and was never to know again" (Book 1). But their much-desired emancipation from parental power and the detested patterns of parental behavior—Billy Pop's self-indulgence and self-pity, the Countess's self-dramatization and selfishly maintained "deep hold on life"—is no simple matter. Sukey has escaped bohemian chaos but replaced it by the domesticity of a devoted mother and a headmaster's wife, and by the whimsy of her broadcasts on family topics like "Winnie the Wolseley": in the process she becomes part of "the Pascoe legend" to her husband's younger staff. Quentin, seeking idealistically to expose first the decadence of capitalism in 1925, then the evils of totalitarian Russia in 1937, finds his way back to newspaper approval by his ability to amuse. He becomes a professional gadfly and a "famous voice" on television (Book 5), unable to love and not reluctant to embrace death in an air crash in 1967. Gladys gains as a businesswoman independence from the father who once molested her and called her "Glad Eyes"; but just as, against her better judgment, she lends the sponging Billy Pop £2 she can ill afford, two decades later, ironically won over by her lover's use of the same endearment, she lends Alfred the proceeds of a painting owned by Jewish refugees, and goes to prison when he fails to pay her back. Rupert, Marcus, and Margaret, reacting strongly against their "awful" parents, nevertheless may be felt to derive much of their talent as actor, collector of paintings, and novelist from the real if less successful authorship of their father, the histrionic appetite for experience and beauty of their mother, and the extravagance of both. As the novel demonstrates the usefulness and the dangers of laughter (a motif already touched on in *The Middle Age of Mrs. Eliot* and *The Old Men at the Zoo*), so it offers through an accumulation of detailed evidence the averaged-out conclusion that the generations of a family resemble each other as much as they differ. The roles taken by the Matthews children in "The Game" are as individually appropriate as their reflections in the "laughing mirrors" are prophetic. Wilson himself has described the novel as "deterministic."[15]

The precise sources of *No Laughing Matter* in Wilson's family past can only be guessed at, but there is no doubt that this past provides much of the "free memory" that gives the novel its emotional conviction. In 1971 Wilson disclaimed any one-to-one similarity between Billy Pop and the Countess and his own parents, while admitting that "certainly the mixture of social pretension and poverty, typical of people in my family, is also typical of the elder Matthews in my novel."[16] In a later interview in 1978 he described his father's habit (fictionalized at the start of Book 3) of decamping from the house, to return sheepishly not long after, and his brothers' habit of acting out that return and the related words of the Wilsons' cook; he also mentioned great family rows.[17] This atmosphere he had already reproduced in his radio play *Skeletons and Assegais*,[18] in which he described his family as "lumpen bourgeois," as Quentin (educated like him at Westminster) does early in Book 3.

In his notes for the novel Wilson listed characteristics of his own that he had divided between the six Matthews siblings, and revealed what is perhaps the deepest personal trigger of the novel in a declaration to the effect that "I have not been destroyed by my humour (or only in some parts and potentially in others)." The two characters in the novel who most resemble him—they are also the most vividly drawn—are Marcus[19] and Margaret, and in their lives the assimilation of humor into a deeper sense of human and social awareness is most fully documented. Margaret struggles in her fiction (an early example of which, her version of Sukey's wedding, is inserted into Wilson's "own" narrative) to relate the necessary "refreshment of negation" (Book 3, part 2) and the coolness of irony with passion, awakened in her brief Mediterranean affair with Clifford Arbuckle, and with "this press of people, this living human mass" (Book 5). Her concern to "mock the mocker" in herself (Book 3, part 3) echoes Wilson's own notes for the novel, in which he speaks of "social observation mocked, and the mockery then mocked to reveal the spiritual failure below." Marcus, with his delightfully "camp" manner, his catty humor, and his "pansy" appearance, reveals more and more beneath them an essential toughness, both in his uncompromising devotion to the best in modern art and in his recognition of responsibility to others: his Jewish lover Jack, opponents of Mosleyite fascism in the 1930s, and finally the Moroccan workers he employs in "Plantagenet Perfumes Ltd," in which his aesthetic and his business interests unite.

No Laughing Matter was greeted by the critics with almost universal praise, and deservedly so. Technically, it is a dazzling performance that never flags; the "palpable weariness" discerned by Bernard Bergonzi[20] in the latter part is not so much a weakening of structural grasp as the natural reflection, manifested in greater brevity of treatment, of the fact that the lives of the Matthews siblings are nearing their end. Marcus and Margaret, sadly misunderstanding one another in the final pages, are yet akin (like the older generation in "Such Darling Dodos") in being about to be shunted aside—as they shunted aside Billy Pop and the Countess—by the visiting grandchildren, Adam and Lucilla, and by Hassan, Marcus's former lover who will inherit his business.

Emotionally (the complex of feelings generated by the final pages is an example) the novel offers a mature, balanced, and moving picture of human life, without ever giving way to the sentimental. The lives of the main characters are particularized with rich invention, skillfully juxtaposed and contrasted in terms of the laughter theme, and given a public resonance by being related to the movement of history—the disillusioned aftermath of World War I, the political polarization of the 1930s, the pressure brought to bear on British insularity and conscience by the influx of Jewish refugees (Frau Liebermann, the Ahrendts, Matthias Birnbaum), the postwar challenge of Suez and its accompaniment, the growth of Arab nationalism (the clash between Jew and Arab kills Sukey's beloved "P.S." in Palestine in the late 1940s). The aging of Billy Pop and the Countess (subsidized by their children since the 1920s) is paralleled by the decline of the country with whose hopes of "Eldorado" they were once, however self-deceivingly, in tune; by the end of the novel only two of their children are still settled in England. Nevertheless, the total effect is not a negative one; closing the book, one feels with Wilson that "it is not time that is the victor but something hard and imperishable . . . in human nature itself."[21] With a strong claim to be considered Wilson's best novel *No Laughing Matter* is certainly a most distinguished culmination to his best fictional decade.

Chapter Seven
Handing on the Torch

Since *No Laughing Matter* the gaps between Wilson's novels have doubled in size, so that in the last sixteen years he has published only two. Both are interesting, and indeed ambitious in their extension of his fictional territory; neither, however, combines its liveliness with the degree of creative grip, the fullness of emotional resonance, that would place it on a level with the best of his previous work.

Outside factors, such as Wilson's involvement, from 1966 to 1973, as a part-time professor at the University of East Anglia in Norwich, and the research, energy, and personal commitment that went into his sizable books on Dickens (1970) and Rudyard Kipling (1977), may have played their part in reducing his output in fiction. But his emphasis, in the two novels he has written, on young people suggests, somewhat in the manner of Shakespeare's last plays, the wish of a mature writer to entrust such hopes of the future as he still entertains to the resilience of the rising generation first presented, in the persons of Adam and Lucilla and their friends, in the final section of *No Laughing Matter*. It is certainly noteworthy that, whereas in his forties Angus Wilson concentrated his first two novels on protagonists aged sixty and more, in his last two, himself aged between sixty and sixty-seven, he has chosen protagonists who at the end of their respective novels are aged twenty-three and twenty-nine.

As If by Magic (1973)

Whereas *No Laughing Matter* covers a long historical range, *As If by Magic* covers a wide geographical one. The larger part of its action takes place abroad, along a trajectory of mostly less developed countries stretching between Morocco and Japan: the "departure via flight" motif that ends Wilson's earliest novels has here been expanded into a full-fledged narrative, partly reflective of his more frequent trips abroad, partly as if to suggest the inefficacy of travel as a mode of escape. If some problems can be left behind, others are bound to be met with. The long, picaresque second book of *As If by*

Magic entitled "The Journeys," mixes documentary with fable as its two main characters travel separately in search of an ideal partner, fleetingly intersect in the discovery of each other, and find their answers respectively in death and in a life of responsible effort in which "magic" is seen as an illusion.

As If by Magic is a novel very much of its period, the end of the 1960s when so many people were seeking panaceas for their and the world's problems, "magics" ranging from the agrarian "green revolution" as applied to less developed countries in Africa and Asia, to eastern mysticism (of the Maharishi Mahesh Yogi variety) as a corrective to the intellectualism of the West; with, in between, cult authors like D. H. Lawrence and J. R. R. Tolkien, and "doing one's thing" sexually. Were it not for Wilson's framing these various topicalities beween an opening fog, reminiscent of Dickens's *Bleak House* and symbolic of human confusion, and a closing commonsensical humanism, thus suggesting a degree of authorial control and judgment, one might feel the novel to be aiming at too "trendy" a success. Certainly much of its raw material—a geisha party and a "gay" bar in Tokyo, a pederastic orgy in Borneo, student discussion in an English Literature seminar, a dispute over the use of a baby's comforter in a hippie commune, a specimen morning at an ashram—does not deserve the amount of attention that goes to making *As If by Magic* Wilson's second-longest novel;[1] and the older reader may from time to time respond in the way that Gerald Middleton did fifteen years earlier:

> He was sick of meeting the sort of people he didn't usually meet in his life and hearing about the sex lives of people who had nothing to do with the sort of life he led.[2]

However, the novelist who wishes to reflect his changing environment must, in the words of W. H. Auden, be willing to "become the whole of boredom" and "suffer dully all the wrongs of man,"[3] and to his general curiosity as a writer of fiction Wilson seems to have added the professor's wish to understand the way his students' minds worked. In his illuminating "Profile of Angus Wilson" Jonathan Raban described a party that Wilson gave in about 1967, at his Suffolk cottage, for staff and students of the University of East Anglia. Through the kitchen window Raban caught sight of Wilson talking to a girl he had discovered messily crying in a corner of his garden, and to Raban there appeared "an odd likeness between them, those two faces in the lit-up room . . . intent and communicative."[4] In this sympathetic reaching across the generations one discerns the germ of Hamo Langmuir, the homosexual plant geneticist who is of Wilson's age-group, and of his goddaughter Alexandra Grant, the twenty-one-year-old student of English Literature at a New University.

Speaking of his novel after it was published, Wilson himself located its genesis in three visual images. One, akin to the scene described by Raban, was of a girl sitting in a classroom at the University of East Anglia after a seminar, "looking absolutely desolate in a huge hat and looking like a 1920s doll that had been thrown into a cupboard."[5] It is in this posture that the newly pregnant Alexandra is found shortly after the start of Book 2, which charts her slow progress from the hermetic prejudices of her own generation to the ability to act sensibly and with determination. The place where she first does so, Goa, is one of those parts of the world in which the visitor's sympathetic impulse to help founders on the stubborn complexity of local attitudes, of the type exemplified in Wilson's second image. A car in which Wilson was traveling in South India swerved to avoid a sacred cow and in doing so ran over rice belonging to old women who sat by the roadside: they suffered this, the loss of their food, more easily than they would have suffered the death of the sacred, inedible cow. The incident is given in Book 2 to Hamo, who, despite being the breeder of a revolutionary high-yield rice appropriately called "Magic," has been unable to help in this instance: the rice run over is "wretched" and "quite unMagical." By this point Hamo's reluctantly growing awareness of life's hopeless cases has inspired in him a despairing sense of human responsibility which is to lead not long hence to his quixotic death. But for much of the Book his eminence as a scientist is balanced, or rather, unbalanced, by his erratic pursuit, idealistic and physical at once, of a "Dream Youth" who will conform to his exacting specifications as to age and physique. This depiction of Hamo grew out of Wilson's third visual image, when he saw a distinguished man "fall over because he was trying to turn round, looking very dignified, while at the same time somehow managing to wink at a page boy in a hotel without being seen."

The mixture in these three ingredients of the serious and the absurd accurately suggests the uncertain tone of *As If by Magic,* which was described by the anonymous reviewer of the *Times Literary Sup-*

plement as Wilson's "noisiest performance so far and his least assured."[6] In part this uncertainty of tone arises from the wide range of cultures and subcultures (youth, homosexual, erstwhile "Angry" like Perry Grant, author of *Above His Station*) that Wilson dips into in his depiction of the human search for "magic" remedies; in part it is due to his choice of a hero and heroine whose proneness, respectively, to farce and to hysteria strain the reader's sympathy for the unhappiness they reveal at other points. But the occurrence toward the end of Book 2 of the word *muddle*—a word associated with the novels of E. M. Forster, and particularly with *A Passage to India*—suggests that the novel's "noise," a matter sometimes of elaborate, self-conscious, even coy verbal textures, sometimes of conversations simply too long for the intrinsic value of what is said, relates to a view of life intended by the author: life as not only an individual's search for meaning, but as a search for love and consequently for communication with others, which is rarely attained. In the large and messy world of *As If by Magic* suffering and tragedy collapse into the ludicrous and gestures across the gaps between people generally miss their aim.

The novel is in three parts, the two outer ones, covering a matter of days and weeks respectively, framing the long central section, which consists of two intercut voyages of discovery, Hamo's spent entirely in the Far East and lasting for a year, Alexandra's lasting for about nine months. Hamo's trip is official, at least in conception: he is to inspect various rice-growing projects, and he expects, as creator of the super-rice variety "Magic," to bask "in the glories of what I have done for the world of rice" (Bk. 1). He is accompanied on his trip by his laboratory assistant Erroll Watton, a shrewd cockney humorist and skilled photographer who is clearly intended by Wilson as a trusty Sam Weller to Hamo's Mr. Pickwick. Grafted on to this Dickensian picaresque, however, is an element from Dostoevsky: the notion of "the divine idiot as hero" (Bk. 2) with which Wilson had flirted as early as *Anglo-Saxon Attitudes* (in the character of the fussy, kindly Frank Rammage) and later toward the end of *The Old Men at the Zoo*. Beneath his public persona as eminent scientist, "the identity he had so carefully constructed over the last years," Hamo is a sad, lonely figure, a homosexual whose one close relationship has failed to survive the modest aging of his lover, Leslie Grant, since when he has enjoyed a succession of short-lived affairs with young men who temporarily inhabit the specifications of his physical ideal. In the East

he hopes to encounter "beauty . . . anonymous, unspoiled by mud-
dying claims of human intimacy," and fondly imagines that "what
could not be understood could be enjoyed unspoiled." Combining
prissy dignity with physical clumsiness, Hamo in his yearning isolation is both ridiculous and touching, a final, eccentric version of the
precarious innocence that Wilson first embodied at length in the
character of Bernard Sands.

Alexandra, his goddaughter and Leslie's niece, is akin to Hamo in
also being a kind of innocent, though in his initial presentation of
her Wilson relies too much on the stereotyped "generation gap." Alienated from her parents, whom she thinks of as "Him" and "Her,"
yet partly dependent on their affection (as is shown at the start of
Book 2, when she temporarily runs away from home), she sees "evil
faces," worries that she may be mad, and at the same time feels it
"stupid and beastly" to be "ordinary." Her activities with a student
mime group, in which she acts a hen, seem a flight from personal
identity rather than a search for it, as does her indulgence in sexual
"tripling" with her two student lovers, the awkward, intuitive Ned
and the elegant, mocking Roderigo. The "tripling" acts out the han-
kerings of D. H. Lawrence at the end of *Women in Love* (Ursula/Bir-
kin/Gerald); to this confusion of literature and life, sincere but
misguided, and leading later to Alexandra's pregnancy, is added her
view of herself, Ned, and Roderigo as three Hobbits from the "in"
book of the 1960s, Tolkien's *Lord of the Rings*. Visiting her parents
just before he leaves on his trip, and sensing the worry and tension
underlying Alexandra's immersion in a "magic" view of life, Hamo
shyly offers her money—a gift of £100 which she hysterically tears
up, insulting him with the nickname "Hamo the Hamster." Apolo-
gizing, she presents him with *her* parting gift, a pair of binoculars:
"magic glasses," equivalent in her mind to the ring that Tolkien's
Frodo takes on his journey, "so that you'll be able to see things more
clearly wherever you go." Both gifts reverberate ironically through
Book 2. Further offerings, each of exactly £100, punctuate Hamo's
travels and are pathetically inadequate to solve the human problems
he meets with (and in part creates); and though Hamo does indeed
see more clearly, the binoculars themselves lead first to the death of
a poor Indian youth to whom he gives them and, soon after, to
Hamo's own death.

Both deaths occur a year later, in Goa, and it is here, in an atmosphere of rising racial and religious tension, that Alexandra and

Hamo briefly meet again. Alexandra, exposed by her pregnancy to the gradual realization that "we aren't protected by magic," and unable to profit from the "sweet and menacing voices" of her elders' advice, has had her baby in Tangier and gone to live, first, at a nearby commune with Ned, Roderigo, and an American student, Elinor, whose ambition it is to rise above the body and the will through Eastern techniques of meditation. Though Alexandra's increasing normality is refreshingly signaled by her declaration, as the others quarrel, that "I won't have my baby mixed up with all this emotional rubbish," she is not ready to opt for marriage with Roderigo, "an uptight misfit" among the hippies, who tries to persuade her that the commune is a "treacle well" and that mere reaction against "middle-class taste and awfulness" isn't enough. While Roderigo returns to England to work for Hamo's great-uncle, the tycoon Sir James Langmuir, Alexandra moves on to Goa: Ned's mime troupe is wanted by the hippy community there, and Elinor wishes to learn from an influential guru, much distrusted by the Catholics of Goa, known as the "Austrian Swami." Through this gross and enigmatic figure Wilson introduces another aspect of the 1960s' search for "magic": the pursuit of occult knowledge, "Lemurian" or "Atlantean" wisdom, associated with prehistoric sites such as Stonehenge and Avebury in England and Msura in Morocco. To Alexandra, the swami is "at least three-quarters charlatan," but Wilson's final view of him, expressed in the Epilogue when the swami refuses to have his gifts exploited by the power-hungry Sir James, is more tolerant: the swami "could doubt at times how much he knew, but he always believed that he had these powers in trust."

Alexandra comes to see the world, finally, as divided into "bullies" (such as Sir James Langmuir and even Roderigo) and "scroungers" (the swami, to some extent, and those members of the hippy community in Morocco who kill for their skins three goats that are the livelihood of local people). When she meets Hamo in Goa, she suddenly sees in him the husband, and father for her child, she has been looking for, someone who has "*never* bullied or cringed," a version of Dostoevsky's "holy fool" Myshkin, who will "make sense of everything." The prospect is half-absurd and, because of Alexandra's boyish, even waiflike appearance, half-attractive to Hamo; but it has no chance of fulfillment. Despite the great success of his "Magic" rice in large areas of the Far East, where it has brought prosperity to many and thus increased trade with the West, he has not always been able to respond in godlike fashion to his creation, as in southwestern Ceylon where "Hamo saw it all and it was very good." He has detected on his travels "a high, distant overtone of perpetual, desperate woe. Could it be the natural noise of the world, as he began to fancy?" His distress has distracted him from the technicalities of his work and given him an obsession with "living conditions, starving poor, exploited masses"; he has even criticized landlordism in the Indian press, provoking the shrewdly misprinted retort: "Go home, Homo." By a bitter irony, the "Most Beautiful Youths" he has encountered in Borneo, India, and Ceylon (the last encounter involving him in the farcical yet poignant deception of the pro-British Jayasekeres, who see in "Dr. Malcolm" from London University a "magic" opportunity of reestablishing contact with England) have all turned out to be the casualties of "magic": dispossessed young men from "hopeless lands" impervious to its cultivation and let fall into neglect. One of these, saving Hamo from entanglement in poisonous seaweed, is drowned by Hamo's clumsy struggles; and a final youth, not "Fair" but thin and ill, to whom Hamo gives his binoculars as "part of a necessary redemption from his past self," is killed by jealous peeping toms and anti-Western vigilantes when he uses them to spy on the naked "heepies" on the beach at Goa: by a final twist of East/West misunderstanding, he has mistaken Elinor's meditation exercises for the sensual movements of lust.

The boy's death decides Hamo not to submit the kind of bland report on his tour that his superiors would prefer. Instead, he recommends a "change of programme": the postponement of research on sorghum (for Africa) in favor of the production of new hybrids suitable for the "hopeless lands"—a long-term effort from which lesser people might benefit, and one that would demonstrate a humanity and goodwill superior to large-scale profit motives. At the same time, he determines to return to Goa, where landless peasants are rioting because they have formed the impression that he is a wonder-working "rice-god" whom the government are keeping from them. Meeting Alexandra, and taking on himself the blame for the situation, Hamo goes out with impressive courage and naive liberal hopefulness to confront an angry mob whose language he does not speak. Predictably, he is killed, the violent manner of his death having about it an element of ritual sacrifice and atonement.

Returning to London (in the Epilogue), Alexandra finds herself Hamo's sole heir and sets herself the task of pressing the suggestions in Hamo's report, a copy of which she finds in his flat. The report is, however, ignored by Sir James Langmuir, the ultimate head of the plant-breeding institute for which Hamo worked. At Hamo's memorial service Sir James presents his death as an object lesson in the hatred of the "weak" and "unteachable" for the "clever" and "strong"; it would be "misguided sentimentalism" to worry about such people. By a final irony, Sir James himself dies of a stroke when the swami, now in England, refuses to admit him to all the occult mysteries his megalomania hopes to make use of, and Alexandra inherits his money also, becoming that Shavian "fictive device," a millionairess. Even with her new riches, though, she lacks the necessary skills to bring Hamo's humanitarian scheme to fruition, and she decides instead to pull down Sir James's enormous tower block, Langmuir House, and build in its place apartments to be let at a loss to people working in the area, so bringing London "nearer to the unique city it could be." Hamo's task cannot be hers, but she will do what she can, "trying to undo the accretion of great wealth by the bullies, looking after the interests of those who haven't yet fallen upon hopeless days."

The future, left open, will require determination and hard work; Alexandra's earnest commitment to it, after her erratic silliness at the start of the novel, provokes admiration. Yet her final, explicit thought—"she knew that no magic spells could solve her problems"—is anticlimactically trite. One is left with the feeling that *As If By Magic* fails to make a satisfying and credible unity out of the many matters and manners, from the topical to the apocalyptic, with which it too strenuously attempts to deal.

Setting the World on Fire (1980)

The world of the super-rich, in which Alexandra finds herself by inheritance at the end of *As If by Magic,* is the world in which Wilson chooses entirely to locate his most recent novel. It is noteworthy how regular a role is played in his novels by the possession, or the acquisition, of adequate private means by the important characters. *Setting the World on Fire* does not, however, occupy Wilson's habitual milieu, that of the comfortable or striving middle classes, but is unique in his work in concerning itself with the aristocracy, both of title and of wealth, a level of society touched on in his previous novels only in such characters as the Godmanchesters in *The Old Men at the Zoo,* Sir

Joseph and Lady Needham, and Sir James Langmuir, in *As If by Magic*. For a novelist writing in England in the 1970s, the choice was a very unusual one, although any element of the "reactionary" is quickly seen to be modified by the novel's emphasis on the proper use of riches. The clue to Wilson's choice may lie in a shift of focus indicated in an interview in 1978: though still liking people, he spoke of a growing boredom with groups of them, and a new interest in "watching bird life and going to look at buildings."[7]

Both interests had appeared in *As If by Magic*. In Goa, Hamo feels momentary delight in looking at cranes and ibises through his "magic glasses"; in the Epilogue Alexandra responds with pleasure to a Wren church in the City of London and plans the future in terms of humane architectural schemes. For someone English (the career of Wilson's near-contemporary Sir John Betjeman is a case in point), an interest in buildings typically connotes, or arises from, the attachment of value to tradition: it frequently takes the form of visiting "great houses," and not unnaturally carries with it a degree of gratitude to those who built them and approval for their descendants who have the responsibility of maintaining them and thus the stability and beauty, of fabric and decoration, that they embody. Such a great house and such a family preside over *Setting the World on Fire*. At its conclusion, in 1969, Wilson adds terrorism—an explosion planned for the Houses of Parliament[8]—to the panorama of the volatile 1960s depicted in *As If by Magic;* but the major part of the novel, which is much exercised by the relationship between creativity and order, asserts positive beliefs which must prevail against destruction and chaos.

Wilson has written at some length, in *The Wild Garden,* of the way in which his imaginative worlds lie like tracing paper over the geography of the real one, so that certain places seem appropriate locations for particular incidents and characters.[9] In practice, this means that his novels satisfy the reader's sense of verisimilitude while retaining their fictional autonomy. Meg Eliot, for instance, is given substance, and precise social ambience, as a character by living in a house in a real street (Lord North Street in Westminster); but one would not expect to find a specific door that was "hers," just as one would not think to encounter Gerald Middleton in Montpelier Square in Knightsbridge. Nor does either case, any more than in Wilson's work generally, do violence to the physical reality of streets and maps. In *Setting the World on Fire* the position is different. Wilson's imaginary family, the Mossons, live in an imaginary "great house" in West-minster, Tothill House; but in addition to being given a history and an architecture of a feasibly "real" kind, it is assigned an exact geographical location, the area between Westminster Abbey and St. John's church in Smith Square—an area in fact occupied by Westminster School (which also figures in the novel) and by mostly residential streets. Instead, that is, of creating a fictional spot that coexists loosely with the real world and so assists a normal "suspension of disbelief," Wilson's imagination has annexed a part of the real world, demolished the buildings on it, and erected one of his own. The sense this makes in terms of story—a tunnel from such a house could lead to the Houses of Parliament—seems insufficient to explain his unusual literalness, which has almost the effect of the "alternate world" convention in science fiction and contributes to the curiously theoretical "feel" of the book. By insisting that the reader see Tothill House[10] where he knows it cannot be, Wilson makes it more shadowy than if left to the geographical approximations of the reader's mind.

One is on more familiar fictional ground with the two main human characters whose importance equals that of Tothill House itself: the brothers Piers and Tom Mosson, who, as teen-agers in the novel's central section, go to a real school. But in presenting the exuberant Piers as the type of the artist—not a writer but a brilliant director of plays—and in sending him to his own school, Westminster, Wilson indirectly offers a clue to his insistence on a precise but untrue location for Tothill House. In the precocious brilliance of Piers, who at age eighteen wins the history scholarship to Christ Church, Oxford, that Wilson missed, and is professionally famous before he is thirty, Wilson projects an idealized version of his own career, which started at age thirty-three; in contriving (through the failure to marry, and later the "squalid" death, of Piers's uncle Sir Hubert Mosson) that Piers, the son of a younger son, shall inherit Tothill House and the Mosson baronetcy, Wilson units the world of art with the world of wealth and privilege into which he himself was not born; and in superimposing Tothill House on the map of Westminster he perhaps recaptures vicariously the stability that a school founded by Elizabeth I represented to a day-boy living amid the transience of small London hotels.

If the success story of Piers, the artist-aristocrat, revises and polishes the outline of his creator's life, many details in the novel recapitulate motifs from his earlier work, the period of whose production is substantially overlaid by *Setting the World on Fire*'s time-span, from 1948 to 1969. This retrospective air seems sometimes the result of a fatigued invention. Rosemary Mosson ("darling heart") and her brother Eustace, Wilson's last "raffish old sport," an author who spends "half the money he never makes" on expensive restaurant meals, recall the Countess and Billy Pop in *No Laughing Matter,* and this much may be unavoidable for a writer with strong family memories.[11] But it seems unnecessary for Rosemary once to have burned her arm (shades of Kay in *Anglo-Saxon Attitudes* and of Bernard's grandson Nicholas in *Hemlock and After*), and functionless in this novel for her to run a nursery garden like David Parker in *The Middle Age of Mrs. Eliot.*

Elsewhere, however, Wilson seems to be collecting elements from earlier novels and short stories, and bringing them to fruition. Piers, learning in 1957 to cope with adults during the casting of the opera *Phaethon* at school, is a more patrician version of Maurice Liebig in "After the Show"; and his successful drawing-out, later, of his great-grandfather, whose long recollection of Great War experiences and romantic first love is for Piers his "only work of art," is both an extension of Geoff's sympathy for his grandfather, Lord Peacehaven, in "Ten Minutes to Twelve" (set at the end of 1956), and the establishment of that rapport across the generations that Alexandra misses with the Needhams in *As If by Magic*. Ralph Tucker, the writer of crude and violent plays, whose smoldering class hostility leads indirectly to the death of Piers's brother Tom, is the nihilistic fulfillment of Tom Pirie, the "angry young" would-be playwright who tries to assault Meg Eliot. And the recurrent image of *Setting the World on Fire,* the legend of Phaethon whose failed, or foiled, attempt to drive the sun-god's chariot symbolizes both artistic ambition and mortal danger in the novel, is the full-scale working out of the phrase used by Lilian Portway in *Anglo-Saxon Attitudes* to describe, with "roguish sadness," Gerald Middleton's arrival at Melpham in 1912: his stumble from the car and his broken ankle make him "Phaeton fallen from his golden chariot."

Nothing in *Setting the World on Fire* could be described as "roguish," nor would "sadness" be an appropriate word for Piers's response to his brother's death at the end (Tom intercepts a bullet meant for Piers, rather as Bill Eliot dies trying to protect the Badai minister in *The Middle Age of Mrs. Eliot*). Centering his novel on the massive architectural splendor of Tothill House, and spreading out to include the painting and opera of the seventeenth century in which it was built, Wilson gives his significant characters—those who love Tothill—something of the larger-than-life quality of personages in the heroic dramas of Corneille, Racine, and Dryden. The claims of ordinary humanity, represented especially by Rosemary Mosson, are given their due in Part 2. When Rosemary at last feels able to admit to her "sweet" mother-in-law Jackie and her snobbish brother-in-law Hubert her long-standing affair with her late husband's friend and comrade-in-arms Jim Terrington, the hostile response she provokes forces Piers and Tom to choose between their grandmother and Tothill, and their mother and exile from it; they choose the latter. But both this family contretemps and the terrorist plot of Part 3, which provides the novel with elements of narrative tension, are subordinate to Piers's development as an artist and to the contrasts between Piers and Tom who, though devoted to each other and, at the end, united against destructive forces, possess different temperaments: the obsessional daring of the creative impulse and an urge to order based on a sense of life's precariousness.

The schematic contrast between the brothers, and the repetition throughout the novel of symbolic motifs and responses which embody it, make *Setting the World on Fire* more like a sequence of formal, balletic tableaux—or perhaps a three-act play—than an intricate, forward-moving story; this impression is heightened, as if the novel were a truncated version of *No Laughing Matter,* by the two ten-year intervals between its sections. Structurally, these three sections are held together by the "Phaethon" motif—first a ceiling painting by Charles II's court painter Antonio Verrio, then an opera by Louis XIV's court composer Lully, first cast, then canceled, and at last put on—and by the Mosson brothers' gradual approach, as child-visitors, as public schoolboys, and as grown men and inheritors, to the "wonderland of Tothill."

Part 1 establishes their characters and their different reactions to Tothill House immediately. Sons of the dead war hero Jerry Mosson, brought to it for the first time in 1948 by their mother, both see, on the high ceiling of the Great Hall, Verrio's painting of Phaethon driving the chariot of the sun-god through the sky, threatening to burn the earth by getting too close, then falling to his death, cast down by Jove to protect mortals from destruction. To eight-year-old Piers, who has just learned to swim, Phaethon's flight and his fall look exhilarating and happy, offering escape from the feeling of being a "beetle" on the marble floor below; six-year-old Tom, dizzied by the Hall's great height, is afraid the ceiling will fall on him and that Phaethon will set the world on fire. Telling him the story of Phaethon, and showing him the difference between such "dangerous fools" and the "level-headed chaps" who stop the "thin ice" of the world from breaking, his uncle Hubert Mosson (a level-headed banker who ironically cherishes a passion for being flagellated, which later leads to his death) introduces him, and the reader, to the two contrasted architects responsible for Tothill House: Sir Roger Pratt, who built a sensible "gentleman's house," orderly and regular, with a central staircase, and Sir John Vanbrugh, who tore out the staircase and replaced it in baroque style by a vast central hall with a domed ceiling and lantern—a splendid but impractical act of "wildness."[12] Throughout the rest of the novel, Piers's taste is for Vanbrugh's portion of Tothill, Tom's for Pratt's, so that they are known to their friends as Van and Pratt. Yet although Piers, impetuous and inventive, knows no fear, and Tom maintains a nervousness about the world's "thin ice" which he pluckily keeps in check, the two brothers are very close to each other and mutually protective. When, in the shrubbery later, Piers's absorbed imitations of their early ancestor Sir Francis Tothill threaten to give their grandmother a bad impression, it is Tom's quickness to notice the danger that gets Piers out of trouble, thus anticipating the end of the book. Their qualities, in fact, are complementary, and though it is Piers, already an impresario at eight and already seeming the natural heir to Tothill, who leads his mother and grandmother back into the Great Hall, he is described as "supported by Tom"—just as he is when he finally inherits.

The same pattern of close friendship based on contrast and similarity continues in Part 2, set in 1956-1957. Piers, now at Westminster School, is directing *Richard II*, whose deposition is compared by Shakespeare to the fall of Phaethon; his brother's personal triumph banishes for a moment Tom's thoughts about thin ice and tightropes over abysses of fire. Later, casting Lully's opera *Phaethon* for performance in the Great Hall of Tothill, and hoping thus to fulfill a frustrated ambition of Vanbrugh's in 1697, Piers discovers what is to be his vocation, the staging of plays. In part, this métier is an extension of his ability to manage the people around him by tact and charm, but essentially it expresses Piers's single-minded, elated concern with the creation of beauty, human happiness, and artistic order: one notices how definite are Piers's views about the opera and the singers suitable to it. Their concern for order is the common ground between the enthusiastic Piers and the cautious Tom (later a lawyer), and although their love for Tothill takes different forms—"objects, values, rooms, purposes" for Tom, "abstract shapes" and "dreams" for Piers—their interdependence is conveyed in Wilson's description of the "Van-Pratt" room in its library, "where order cradled aberration, and baroque imposed regularity."[13]

Disorder enters the novel with Marina Luzzi, Hubert Mosson's "jet-set" Italian fiancée, the young widow of a high-ranking, executed Fascist. Congratulating Piers on *Richard II,* she prophesies, correctly, that "in the theatre you would set the world on fire." It is she who suggests, imperiously, the performance of *Phaethon* at Tothill which, as a result of great-grandfather Mosson's death and consequent family divisions, does not in fact take place—an instance of the uncertainties of life, ever-menacing to Tom, which Piers, hoping to fly like Phaethon (Bk. 2, Chap. 7), is unable to control. Piers at first admires "the Luzzi" 's style and panache: "a crazy lady with a power urge is just what I need so long as I keep an eye on her antics," he remarks to Tom at the *Phaethon* auditions, in a phrase pregnant with authorial irony. Tom, however, has at first sight recognized her as a person "out of order . . . unconcerned with order," a view which by the end of Part 2, when she suddenly abandons her engagement to Hubert and her tug-of-war with Jackie Mosson for him and Tothill, Piers comes to share. Marina's vitality is fundamentally destructive, her wish to "set the world on fire" no metaphor: for her, most things in life are "boaring" and "chaos is the only exciting thing left." She stands at the opposite end of the psychological spectrum from Tom; Piers, for whom even the baroque art of "Vanbrugh at his most fantastic" is "based upon order," stands creatively at the center, and when at the novel's conclusion, melodramatic but symbolically persuasive, Tom dies in preventing Marina from shooting his brother, the opposites cancel out, leaving Piers as the survivor, lonely, aware now of the dangers of life's thin ice, but still courageous.

With poignant irony, Tom's death occurs just when he has "begun shamelessly to enjoy things," an enjoyment brought about by living at Tothill again and by falling in love with the soprano, "enduring" and "reliable," who has sung the part of Théone in *Phaethon.* Piers, having inherited "Tothill's magnificence" on his uncle Hubert's death, and having meanwhile gained an international reputation in the theater, has at last fulfilled his boyhood wish to put on *Phaethon* at Tothill. With experience, his "assertive certainty of genius" has turned into "modest prayer for recognition"; yet he remains certain that a director's "homage" to the work he stages must carry with it a burning ambition equivalent to, and thus worthy of, that of its creator. It is through an act of combined miscalculation and hubris—going on to produce at Tothill an "oddly conventional" historical play by its steward, Ralph Tucker, whose underlying "emotional force" he does not grasp—that Piers lets in the "political madness" that in the late 1960s is interfering with "such real things as the arts" but that also bears out Jackie Mosson's words twelve years earlier: "Half the world now wants to bring down the rich and secure." Ralph's play, involving the Gunpowder Plot, is merely a device to enable him to gain access, during its preparations, to Parliament; police vigilance on the first night (puzzling to Piers) defeats the plan, but Tom's death pays for Phaethon's error.[14]

In an interview in 1978 Wilson described himself as having three aspects:

I walk on thin ice, and I pray that the ice will stick, and I think three things: I think how marvellous ordered life is . . . Then I think, Oh, if I could only get away from this ordered life to the wild. And then I think, Oh, God help us—the best thing is if we'd all blow up.[15]

Setting the World on Fire turns these aspects into Tom, Piers (in a sense), and Marina Luzzi. In the book's unusually eloquent final paragraph Marina's nihilism is transposed into the feeling of precariousness and panic that seizes Piers when he returns across Westminster Bridge after his brother's death in hospital:

The water flowing below, the starred sky above him, seemed ready to meet, to burst upon the human insects, upon him, in one shapeless flow of eternity. . . . What good were his wonderful Vanbrugh inventions in a dead, chaotic universe?

In realizing this emptiness, in feeling for the first time a fear of falling, Piers repeats in his own experience the terror felt by Tom, crossing Hungerford Bridge twelve years before (Part 2, chap. 6.) But in thus becoming his brother, and at last recognizing life as dangerous, Piers is able heroically to reassert his last promise to Tom: to "do his own thing," to continue as an artist and, like Ibsen's Master Builder—the play he is currently directing—"go up, go up," whatever the risks. Whether the very last phrase—"Lest delaying, you lose the power to ascend the towers of imagination"—is Wilson's dare to himself and presages further novels, it is impossible to say. Be that as it may, *Setting the World on Fire*, whatever its limitations as a "realistic" novel,[16] is a powerful and absorbing study of the creative impulse, a noble assertion of the artist's role, and of the truth and beauty he serves, in an unstable and often menacing world.

Chapter Eight
Ocelots and Jaguars

The exuberant conservatism of *Setting the World on Fire,* in which an aristocratic and wealthy milieu is associated with the necessity of order and the generosity of creative art, seems appropriately coincidental with the knighthood that Wilson was awarded in 1980, the year of its publication. Its revival, in effect, of the Victorian novel of high life, and its celebration of the high art—opera, architecture, plays elaborately staged—which requires time, money and patronage, bring into prominence Wilson's differences from the "angry young" novelists, the "kitchen sink" dramatists (themselves admittedly changed by 1980) with whom he shared the latter part of his first decade as a writer, and with whose work his own apparent "satire" of middle-class mores was for a time connected.

To accept an equivalence, however, between Wilson and his younger contemporaries in the 1950s is to succumb to one of the occupational hazards of the literary historian, who as the past recedes is apt to blur the precision of single years into the time scale of a whole decade. The emergence of Wilson as a sharp yet compassionate observer of the postwar social melting-pot occurred in 1949, a moment, as Ian Scott-Kilvert correctly noted eleven years later, "when the scene was uncommonly bare of new talent."[1] The waves made by Wilson's arrival were powerful enough to cross the Atlantic within a year, causing the American critic Edmund Wilson almost to brush aside a still-active senior in the enthusiasm of his greeting: "After Evelyn Waugh, what? For anyone who has asked this question, the answer is Angus Wilson."[2] By 1952 Wilson had consolidated his reputation with two books of short stories and his first novel *Hemlock and After,* which blended sympathy with prewar liberal humanism and courageous frankness about homosexuality, a subject hardly touched on by British writers hitherto.[3] Of this novel the *Times Literary Supplement* commented that "in his picture of modern English life [Wilson] seizes on fashions in thought and in speech that have not been noted before, and are recognized for the first time with a shock of recognition."[4] Thus Wilson had established his individuality as a writer and won himself an audience well before the appearance of John Wain's misfit hero Charles Lumley, in *Hurry on Down* in 1953, and the impressive debuts of Kingsley Amis, William Golding, and Iris Murdoch in 1954.[5] Nor were these, or later emerging writers, to eclipse him in critical esteem. In 1959 he figured in the *Times Literary Supplement* in a list of "the four leading British novelists of the period,"[6] the other three being Golding, Murdoch, and Lawrence Durrell, the first novel of whose "Alexandria Quartet," *Justine,* had been published in 1957. In 1962 the American critic James Gindin pronounced him "the best contemporary English novelist,"[7] a view he reiterated in 1967.[8]

Wilson shared with a number of novelists of the 1950s, Amis and Wain among them but notably C.P. Snow, a reaction against the fictional experiments of earlier writers such as Joyce and Woolf, with their diminished emphasis on narrative and on moral discriminations and their greater concern for the rendering of individual consciousness by means of extensive interior monologue. Where the style of C.P. Snow, the first novel of whose sequence "Strangers and Brothers" appeared in 1949, prompted comparisons with Trollope, Wilson acknowledged indebtedness to Dickens, whom he had first read at the age of eleven and from whom he gained the taste for long novels evidenced by five of his own, and to Emile Zola, on whom he published a critical study in 1952. Many of the traits of Zola noted there resemble elements in Wilson's own work which were explicitly glossed in 1963 in *The Wild Garden*: Zola's use of animals as symbols, his painstaking preparatory work to guarantee his novels' factual and atmospheric accuracy, his response to "the stresses placed upon his emotions in childhood and adolescence," his awareness of "the dreadful gulf that lies between his fantasy world . . . and the vast, uncomforting desert of the society in which he must live."[9]

One must, however, emphasize Wilson's differences from Snow and from the "angry young men." Unlike Snow, Wilson even in the 1950s was far more tolerant of writers such as William Golding who were "swimming against the tide" of the neo-traditionalism he then favored: "Orthodoxy of the social novel . . . would be as deplorable as the orthodoxy of Bloomsbury."[10] Like Simon Carter's at the end of *The Old Man at the Zoo,* Wilson's footing in the postwar literary world carried with it an appreciative awareness of the prewar one, which in the 1960s took the form of an admiration for both Joyce and Woolf, and an attempt, in 1963, to rescue from "monstrous neglect" the massive novels of John Cowper Powys, with their mixture of detailed realist observation and ambitious dionysiac fantasy.[11] Indeed, Wilson's devotion to Dickens (on whom he produced in 1970 an energetic study which, like his later book on Kipling, gives as much the impression of total "by heart" recall as of industrious research) stems not simply from Dickens's realism, his response to the pressures of the Victorian age, but from his embodiment in fiction of strong obsessional drives, his interest in "the dangerous edge of things,"[12] akin to Wilson's own fascination with the "thin ice" separating order from chaos, and his broad imaginative scope. Wilson made clear in 1963 the combined elements in his own work, and his ultimate preference:

I have never felt called upon to declare allegiance to either fantasy or realism. They proceed from two different levels of imagination and without their fusion I could not produce a novel. However, if I must choose between two necessities I should consider the "real" as the less essential. (WGa, 137)

Wilson's difference from many of his publishing contemporaries is well conveyed by a comment he made in 1957, when interviewed by Michael Millgate. Asked for his views on the "angry young men," he replied with an old-fashioned courtesy that carried with it, at the end, a distinct note of reproof for their apparent unwillingness to attend to one of the responsibilities of their craft, the responsibility not to undervalue human potential and, it seems implied, by so doing degrade the writer's role:

. . . they are so concerned to say they won't be taken in . . . that one sometimes wishes they'd be a bit more hypocritical. After all, if you think of yourself in that way you come to think of everything else in that way and reduce everything to the level of a commercial traveller talking in a bar, knowing life only too well . . . It isn't quite good enough for serious artists.[13]

It is appropriate in defining Wilson's position to point out one combination of personal factors that links him not with his publishing contemporaries but with many writers whose careers began before World War II, including some of those in the Bloomsbury milieu against which he was in "great reaction"[14] in the 1950s. Wilson was unique among the "new" novelists of the 1950s in coming from an upper-middle-class background and going to both a major public school and an "old" university. Whatever some of his theoretical attitudes, such as his view of the limitations of Forsterian humanism, the perspective on life and art conveyed by his creative work is based on instinctive assumptions not shared by his juniors. He himself has spoken of learning from Proust—hardly a simple "realist" influence— a sense of "paradox and the truth of improbability";[15] he has tried, if not often successfully, for the spiritual reach of Dostoevsky, as well as for the moral seriousness of George Eliot and Jane Austen (all of them novelists much admired by "Bloomsbury"); and the American critic Arthur Edelstein, in a most perceptive essay on *Late Call,* has described him as "a novelist more clearly in the line of Henry James than perhaps anyone else writing today."[16]

In 1964, with only four novels so far available for critical consideration, Wilson was the youngest novelist to form the subject of a study (by Jay L. Halio) in the recently started *Writers and Critics* series; he was also described by Walter Allen, in his survey *Tradition and Dream,* as "the most ambitious novelist in British English since the war," who had "attempted to bring back into fiction the amplitude and the plenitude of the Victorians."[17] Favorable response to the solidity and human concern of his fiction was, however, accompanied by strictures. While feeling "interest and respect," G. S. Fraser put his finger on a genuine lack in most of Wilson's work: "I can think of no living novelist with less of the poet in him."[18] If "poetry" is taken to mean a sense of the numinous, the mysterious, or simply the beautiful, as this is found in the fiction of, for example, Forster, Virginia Woolf, or William Golding, Wilson shows little of it, though Gerald Middleton's drive to Melpham in 1912, Simon Carter's response to badgers, Sylvia Calvert's to her escape from childhood chores and later to the countryside around Carshall, and Piers Mosson's excitement at the architecture of Vanbrugh constitute exceptions. If by "poetry" one means the frisson of words strikingly chosen or combined, cadences that give the reader pause, or the spareness of unhurried sentences, these too are discovered only rarely in Wilson's crowded paragraphs: as Fraser also pointed out, Wilson "is a vigorous and clear writer, but his prose has not the distinction and balance of Waugh and Powell."[19] Fraser's criticisms are just, but it is significant that few commentators have echoed them; in anticipating Fraser in 1960, Ian Scott-Kilvert indicated the reason why this should be so:

His descriptive style has always been the least impressive element in his writing . . . in the wider spaces of the novels his expression, never particularly graceful, lapses all too easily into clichés, redundant phrases and

overloaded metaphors. It is a tribute to Mr. Wilson's narrative power that
the eye so often passes over these defects and that he is praised for the com-
pulsively readable quality of his prose.[20]

"Narrative power" and compulsive readability were not quite
enough for Anthony Burgess, writing in 1965 about the contribution
made by Wilson and by C.P. Snow to the postwar traditionalist
novel. Himself a composer of music, admirer of Joyce, and experi-
menter with language (in *A Clockwork Orange* of 1962), Burgess
damned them with faint praise: "In the age of Boulez both are content with the technique of Brahms."[21] Were this statement true of
Wilson, one might adequately retort by pointing out that Brahms's
technique created Brahms's music; but in fact it was not, Wilson
having already, in *The Old Men at the Zoo*, grafted fable on to realism
from a "feeling that the traditional form was inhibiting me from saying all that I wanted to say."[22] One may interject at this point, however, that throughout his career Wilson's response to his own
technical needs, and to the pressure of those personal concerns bred
in the loneliness and isolation necessary to most writers,[23] may well
have been tinged, since he has also been a very public man of letters,
with a responsive awareness of the contemporary literary context.[24] It
is possible, for instance, to see in *Late Call* Wilson's version of the
lower-class provincial-life novel current from the mid-1950s; in *The
Old Men at the Zoo* an expression of the human tendency to evil demonstrated in Golding's *Lord of the Flies* (1954); and certainly in *As If
by Magic* a touch of the professor proving his alertness by registering
the cults and cult-authors of his students.[25] But it would be unfair to
call this more than an openness to fresh possibilities, and the results,
with the partial exception of *As If by Magic,* have justified any
intentions.

Wilson's adoption, as it may seem, of "the technique of Boulez"
in *No Laughing Matter* (1967) has provoked in the period since then
an emphasis in critical discussion of him strikingly different from
what preceded it, so that this novel, standing at the midpoint of his
career so far, can easily seem a turning point also. Before it, he was
generally seen as neo-Victorian in manner, his matter the tensions
between the individual and society and the plight of the humanist in
a world growing more violent and insecure; with it he is viewed as
sophisticated and modern (an image he has encouraged by speaking
of his admiration for Beckett, Borges, and Nabokov), undermining
the reality of his characters and their environments by techniques of

reader-alienation—the "Chinese Box" effect of Margaret Matthews's "Carmichael stories," extensive use of literary parodies, switches from narrative to dramatic method, and in *As If by Magic* what A.S. Byatt has recently called "farcical fictiveness," the reduction of "everything to the ridiculous in an intensely, inexorably, exclusively literary way."[26] Malcolm Bradbury, writing in 1973, was even prompted to see all Wilson's previous novels in the light of the "strange positional insecurities" revealed by Wilson's new "narrative posture" of 1967:

> Wilson's six apparently substantial and stable novels, socially panoramic and dense, do not in fact hold steady when we read them, but dissolve into a distinctive type of grotesque.[27]

Nevertheless, though Bradbury's comment, made from a more "up-to-date" theoretical standpoint, does justice to the mixed effect Wilson's novels indeed have, Wilson's blurring of realism into fable was felt, if not named as such, by the earliest critics of *Hemlock and After,* in the uneasy coexistence of Bernard Sands, a credibly "realistic" character, and Mrs. Curry, an ectoplasmic manifestation of evil. In addition, it is difficult to say whether the cast lists that precede five of Wilson's novels (from *Hemlock* to *Setting the World on Fire*) are not as much a relic of nineteenth-century fiction as they may be a distancing device appropriate to novels less convinced of their rootedness in fictional "reality"—itself a phrase which returns the critic to traditional ideas about the "suspension of disbelief" involved in any work of literature. And the diversification of *No Laughing Matter* by means of "The Game" and various playlets, some of them employing asides to the reader-"audience," need have their origin in nothing more epistemologically suggestive than the memories of a middle-class child taking part in family or school charades. The critic who seems most sensibly to relate *No Laughing Matter* to the rest of Wilson's literary career is Valerie Shaw, who, writing in 1970, saw it as both a continuation and an extension of his interests, as an intelligent artist and as a humane being:

> . . . the traditional writer who enmeshes in his art a sense of its very difficulties is not . . . changing his spots by putting on some sort of "experimentalist" disguise. He is simply increasing the range of experience with which his fiction deals, and if the relations between art and reality enter the narrative stream they do not therefore sacrifice their thematic status to considerations of pure form.[28]

As Jonathan Raban noted in 1974, "there's always a danger of making Wilson sound more theoretical, more of a *nouveau romancier*, than he is."[29] Wilson himself, in 1978, denied the presence in his work of "abstract thought," saying that "Life in the particular is how I see it very much," and indicating his hope that in his novels readers would find both "a world of people" and "a world of things." "What I want," he concluded, "is for people to say 'Your novel seems very total.' "[30] Wilson's novels constitute, in fact, an ambitious attempt, more often successful than not, to embody the complexity of life by combining acute social observation with strong moral concern. Perhaps his most salient characteristic as a writer is a voracious curiosity and tolerance, expressed both in his depiction of a wide range of human types and the various worlds, animate and inanimate, against which they try to define themselves, and as a remarkably varied repertoire of techniques.

Beneath his technical brilliance Wilson is deeply aware of the difficulty of the human condition and, "enormously," of the isolation of being a writer. He conceded in 1974, somberly, that his novels strike "a slight note of affirmation,"[31] but felt that each of them has progressively made "greater demands on my readers and [shed] the people who felt they got it all last time." Against this somewhat depressed "inside" view, one must set the total of Wilson's impressive achievement, a body of work that, in one critic's words, fulfills an important "requirement of art—that it should help people lead their lives."[32] Its distinct character may fairly be indicated by a further remark by Wilson himself:

You know, one says, "We're both writers"; well, that's true, but it's like an ocelot and a jaguar sitting together and saying "we're both fellidae," you know? I haven't got many contemporaries.[33]

Nor, in the world of the postwar British novel, has Wilson many equals, either in scope or in accomplishment; and those who may be considered his equals—Golding, Murdoch, Burgess—do not disturb his unique position as a writer who has maintained the social relevance and moral authority of the novel while extending its capacity to challenge and entertain the reader's imagination.

Notes and References

Chapter One

1. Wilson in conversation with the author, 20 January 1981.
2. Wilson, interview by Michael Millgate, *Paris Review,* 1957. Reprinted in *Writers at Work,* ed. Kay Dick (Harmondsworth: Penguin Books, 1972), 54; hereafter cited as Millgate interview.
3. Peter Faulkner, *Angus Wilson: Mimic and Moralist* (London: Secker & Warburg, 1980), 12.
4. *The Wild Garden* (London, 1963), 90; hereafter cited in text as *WG* followed by page number.
5. "Bexhill and After," *Spectator,* 9 May 1958, 583.
6. *The Strange Ride of Rudyard Kipling* (New York, 1977), 301.
7. "Skeletons and Assegais," *Transatlantic Review* 9 (Spring 1962).
8. *The Strange Ride of Rudyard Kipling,* 185.
9. "Bexhill and After," 583.
10. *The Strange Ride of Rudyard Kipling,* 318.
11. *As If by Magic* (London, 1973), 389.
12. See Betsy Draine, "An Interview with Angus Wilson," *Contemporary Literature* 21 1 (1980) 3–4.
13. John Carleton, *Westminster School: A History* (London; Rupert Hart-Davis, 1938), rev. ed. (1965), p. 88.
14. "Bexhill and After," p. 584.
15. Their flavor is indicated in Wilson's radio play "Skeletons and Assegais," reprinted in *Transatlantic Review* 9 (Spring 1962): 37.
16. Ibid.
17. Essay in *My Oxford,* ed. Ann Thwaite (London: Robson Books, 1977), 102; hereafter cited in text as *MO* followed by page number.
18. Jay L. Halio, *Angus Wilson* (Edinburgh, 1964), 7.
19. In *Writers at Work: The Paris Review Interviews,* ed. Malcolm Cowley, (New York: Viking Press, 1959), 254.
20. "World's Greatest Museum," *Holiday,* September 1955, p. 52.

Chapter Two

1. *Times* (London) *Literary Supplement,* 26 March 1949.
2. Millgate interview, 63.
3. Ibid.
4. Elizabeth Bowen's collected short stories were published in London, by Jonathan Cape, in 1980, with an introduction by Angus Wilson.

5. "The Short Story Changes," *Spectator* 198 (1 October 1954): 401.

6. Ibid.

7. Kingsley Amis, "Dodos on the Wing," *Spectator*, 18 October 1957.

8. Wilson uses this phrase in *The Wild Garden*, p. 38.

9. June F. Mercer, "Trifle Angus Wilson," reprinted in *New Statesman Competitions*, ed. Arthur Marshall (London: Turnstile Press, 1955), 71.

10. See *The Wild Garden*, 36–37.

11. Halio, *Angus Wilson*, 18.

12. *Times* (London) *Literary Supplement*, 26 March 1949.

13. Millgate interview, 59.

14. *The Wrong Set* (London, 1949), 38–39; hereafter cited in the text as *WS* followed by page number.

15. This is Jay L. Halio's term *(Angus Wilson*, 14) for the recurrent type (Trevor Cawston, Bruce Talfourd-Rich) in Wilson's fiction, a type deriving considerably from Wilson's father.

16. Review of *The Wrong Set*, *Times* (London) *Literary Supplement*, 26 March 1949.

17. J.D. Scott, review of *The Wrong Set*, *New Statesman & Nation*, 30 April 1949, 452.

18. The phrase evokes the hard-bitten line of a wartime Royal Air Force song: "They scraped him off the runway like a pound of strawberry jam."

19. Millgate interview, 58.

20. Wilson in conversation with the author, 20 January 1981.

21. Ibid.

22. Ibid. The "blue silk" gowns worn by the scholars is a transposed reference to the famous red gowns uniquely worn by St. Andrews undergraduates.

23. "The Short Story Changes," *Spectator*, 1 October 1954, 402.

24. Review of *Such Darling Dodos*, *Times* (London) *Literary Supplement*, 28 July 1950.

Chapter Three

1. Frederick P.W. McDowell, "An Interview with Angus Wilson," *Iowa Review* 3, no. 4 (Fall 1972): 83; hereafter cited as McDowell interview.

2. K. W. Gransden, *Angus Wilson* (London, 1969), p. 7.

3. Evelyn Waugh, review of *Hemlock and After*, *Month* (London) 8 (1952): 238.

4. *The Wild Garden* (Los Angeles, 1963), 147; hereafter cited in text as *WGa* followed by page numbers.

5. The manuscripts of Wilson's novels, as well as of most of his other works, were acquired in 1968 by the University of Iowa.

6. *Hemlock and After* (London, 1952), 15; hereafter cited in text as *HA* followed by page number.

7. Wilson's original title for the first chapter.

8. Apart from Zola's involvement with the Dreyfus case, which irritated the French political establishment, one should note Wilson's description of him in later life: "the spare academic figure with beard, pincenez and bicycling knickerbockers" (*Emile Zola,* [London 1952], 81). On the first page of *Hemlock* Bernard talks of the "histrionic dangers" of his position, "the knickerbockered, bearded, self-satisfied, quizzing air."

9. Stephen Wall, *The Sphere History of English Literature,* vol. 7 (The Twentieth Century), ed. Bernard Bergonzi (London: Sphere Books, 1970), 259.

10. For a fictional version of the effect of the Festival in the provinces, cf. J. B. Priestley's novel *Festival at Farbridge* (London: Heinemann, 1951).

11. The phrase is used in the entry on Socrates in the *Encyclopaedia Brittannica.*

12. In 1953 Lord Montagu of Beaulieu, in a celebrated case, was imprisoned for homosexual offenses; and the actor Sir John Gielgud was fined for importuning. Both incidents are referred to in a letter from Evelyn Waugh to Nancy Mitford, 22 October 1953. See *The Letters of Evelyn Waugh,* ed. Mark Amory (London: Weidenfeld & Nicolson, 1980, 411–12).

13. Gransden, *Angus Wilson,* 9.

14. McDowell interview, 82.

15. See "Mythology in John Cowper Powys's Novels," *A Review of English Literature* 4, no. 1 (January 1963): 9.

16. It is significant of Wilson's hostility to Hubert that Gransden (*Angus Wilson,* 11) speaks of Elsie, incorrectly, as a thirteen-year-old girl. The British age of consent is 16.

17. J. D. Scott, *New Statesman and Nation,* 2 August 1952, p. 142.

18. McDowell interview, 82.

19. The manuscript refers specifically to "St. Roland's College, Cambridge," the university with which most members of the Bloomsbury Group were connected.

20. *The Mulberry Bush* (London, 1956), 99; hereafter cited in text as *MB* followed by page number.

21. Millgate interview. "A Bit Off the Map" is, in part, a satirical presentation of the group of young writers associated with Colin Wilson, whose book *The Outsider* (1956) was dedicated to Angus Wilson.

22. *A Bit off the Map* (London, 1957), 61.

Chapter Four

1. Millgate interview, 91.

2. In Wilson's notes for the novel, its earliest title was "Perfect and Pluperfect"; a later possibility was "Saxon Side-Tracks."

3. The real Eorpwald mentioned in Bede's *Ecclesiastical History* was an Anglo-Saxon king.

4. The novel's title (amplified in its epigraph) is taken from chapter 7 of Lewis Carroll's *Through the Looking Glass* (1871).

5. G. S. Fraser, *The Modern Writer and His World* (Harmondsworth: Penguin, 1964), 152.

6. *Anglo-Saxon Attitudes* (London, 1956), 5; hereafter cited in text as *ASA* followed by page number.

7. Wilson is inconsistent about Gerald's age: once he is 62, twice he is 60, but most usually he is (or can be calculated to be) 64. In Wilson's early notes for the novel he is (under the name Theodore Livesey) 65.

8. Millgate interview, 95.

9. This sort of title had been used by Wilson in his earliest notes for *Hemlock and After*. Its unwritten precursor, "Power and Affection," had been divided into four books, entitled "View and Death," "Hue and Cry," "Faith and Works," "Judgement and Costs."

10. Millgate interview, 100.

11. Anthony Rhodes, *Listener*, 17 May 1956.

12. Millgate interview, 95.

13. Review, *Times* (London) *Literary Supplement*, 21 November 1958.

14. Goronwy Rees, *Listener*, 27 November 1958.

15. Wilson had originally thought of Meg's having three children.

16. Martin Green, "Artist Astray," *Chicago Review* 12, no. 3 (Autumn 1958): 77.

17. *The Middle Age of Mrs. Eliot* (London, 1958), 62; hereafter cited in text as *MA* followed by page number.

18. The "Virginia Woolf" element is overdone: among the guests at Meg's party are a couple called "the Pargiters"—the family dealt with in Virginia Woolf's *The Years* (1936).

19. The name is intended to sound pretentious; it derives from Anderida, the name for the much larger forested area stretching across Surrey and Kent in Roman times.

20. There was considerable interest, in 1950s England, in communities organized on religious or quasi-religious lines. In the same year (1958) as *The Middle Age of Mrs. Eliot* Iris Murdoch published *The Bell*, with its "Imber Court" lay-religious community. Wilson referred to it in *The Wild Garden* (138), as a "fine novel."

Chapter Five

1. John Wain, *Observer* 24 (September 1961): 30.

2. McDowell interview, 89.

3. Quoted from Wilson's notebooks for "Goat and Compasses" in the library of the University of Iowa.

4. Reprinted in four successive issues of *Listener*, 27 December 1962 to 17 January 1963.

5. Wilson's notes are perhaps revealing here: Simon was first envisaged as 52, then as 48 (with an American wife aged 35). Wilson was 47 when he wrote the novel.

6. McDowell interview, 91.

7. This and the two previous quotations are from Wilson's notes for *The Old Men at the Zoo*, held in the library of the University of Iowa.

8. The acquisition of sea water from the Bay of Biscay was actually carried out, before World War II, by Charles Vinall, overseer of London Zoo's aquarium. The information (in L. R. Brightwell, *The Zoo Story* [London: Museum Press, 1952], 226) was part of Wilson's sizable research on the background of his novel.

9. McDowell interview, 95.

10. *The Old Men at the Zoo* (London, 1961), 160; hereafter cited in text as *OMZ* followed by page number.

11. Harriet's sexual involvement with her German Shepherd dog, Rickie, which leads it to savage her, seems intended as a grim, extreme object lesson in human/animal rapprochement, and thus to reinforce one of the novel's themes. But the dog's reaction (a kind of "shaggy dog story"?) is surely too extreme to be credible, though Wilson presents it as genuine (*The Wild Garden*, 112).

12. Animal terms are used throughout by Carter to describe various characters. The device serves two somewhat contradictory purposes: both to emphasize the closeness of the human world to the animal, and to indicate Simon's sometimes frivolous avoidance of a full response to good and bad human characteristics alike.

13. This is held in the library of the University of Iowa.

14. See A. J. P. Taylor, *English History 1914–1945* (Oxford: Clarendon Press, 1965), 398.

15. McDowell Interview, 90.

16. *Letters of Evelyn Waugh*, 574–75.

Chapter Six

1. *Listener*, 19 November 1964.

2. Wilson researched this very carefully: his Notes record the maximum sun hours for the July and August of 1909 to 1913. The July of 1911 had practically no rain, and a third more sun hours (334.3) than its nearest rival, August 1909.

3. *Late Call* (London, 1964), 19; hereafter cited in text as *LC* followed by page number.

4. See McDowell interview 96, which makes it clear that some readers did not make the connection between Sylvia Calvert and the Prologue.

5. The words, of course, are used by Linda Loman of her husband

Willy; but they clearly sum up Miller's own view of the value of his ordinary characters.

6. One is presumably also meant to have in mind "call" as "vocation," and William Law's famous treatise of 1729, *Serious Call to a Devout and Holy Life.*

7. See McDowell interview, 81–82. Wilson's intention, in using fake quotations, was to contrast the meaningless cultural tags of cosmopolitan Europe with the more limited, but genuine experience of Sylvia Calvert; but none of the critics noticed, and one is not surprised.

8. *Clayhanger* (1910), *Hilda Lessways* (1911), *These Twain* (1915).

9. *No Laughing Matter* (London, 1967), 44; hereafter cited in text as *NLM* followed by page number.

10. Something of this earlier attitude is recapitulated in Draine, "An Interview with Angus Wilson," 11.

11. McDowell interview, 98.

12. Ibid., 101.

13. Ibid., 99.

14. "Laughing Mirrors" was Wilson's original title for the novel.

15. McDowell interview, 103.

16. Ibid., 99.

17. Draine interview, 4.

18. Reprinted in *Transatlantic Review* 9 (Spring 1962).

19. Compare the description of Marcus early in Book 1 to the photograph of Angus Wilson playing croquet as an Oxford undergraduate, in *My Oxford* (London: Robson Books, 1977).

20. Bernard Bergonzi, *The Situation of the Novel* (London, 1972), p. 188.

21. McDowell interview, 105.

Chapter Seven

1. Some pages omitted from Book 1, concerned with Perry and Zoe Grant, Alexandra's parents, were published as "Untitled," in *Iowa Review* 3, no. 4 (Fall 1972): 106–108.

2. *Anglo-Saxon Attitudes,* Part 2, chap. 2, 327.

3. W. H. Auden, "The Novelist" (December 1938), in *The English Auden* (London: Faber & Faber, 1977), 238.

4. Jonathan Raban, "Profile of Angus Wilson," *New Review* 1, no. 1 (1974): 17.

5. C. C. Barfoot, "Interview with Angus Wilson," *Dutch Quarterly Review of Anglo-American Letters* 6, 4 (1976): 283.

6. *Times* (London) Literary Supplement, 1 June 1973.

7. Draine interview, 13.

8. This is casually anticipated in *As If By Magic* (Bk. 2), when Mar-

tin Abdy accuses Leslie of speaking to his niece Alexandra "as though she'd been trying to blow up Parliament."

9. See *The Wild Garden* (1963), 118–37.

10. The house's name, like that of the family who built it, is drawn from Tothill Street opposite Westminster Abbey, as if to reinforce the likeliness of its location.

11. Two transpositions of these occur in the novel. Jackie Mosson, like Wilson's mother, is a Christian Scientist. Rosemary finally settles in Umtali, Rhodesia—a return, slightly modified by Wilson's liberalism, to his mother's South African origins.

12. Sir Roger Pratt designed and built Coleshill House in Berkshire (1650–1662), then went on to build his masterpiece, much imitated for the rest of the century, Clarendon House in Piccadilly, London (1664–67). It was pulled down in 1683. Sir John Vanbrugh, the playwright and architect (1664–1726), designed Blenheim Palace, Castle Howard, and Seaton Delaval Hall in Northumberland. Wilson's Tothill House is an imaginary, smaller version of Pratt's very symmetrical Clarendon House, with Vanbrugh's Great Hall and lantern at Castle Howard grafted on to it. How well—despite the differences between Pratt and Vanbrugh—the two styles complement each other can be seen by comparing the engraving of Clarendon House in Mark Girouard, *Life in the English Country House* (1978), (Harmondsworth: Penguin Books, 1980), 127, with photographs of Castle Howard: a particularly suitable one is in the AA *Treasures of Britain* (London: Drive Publications, 1968), p. 129.

13. *Setting the World on Fire* (London, 1980), 77.

14. The strong feeling that infuses Wilson's depiction of Piers and Tom (who represent, separately, characteristics united in himself) has perhaps a family origin. Cf. *The Wild Garden* (1963), 140: "As a child I was much with my brother next in age—13 years old when I was born. He was a youth of exceptional powers, strangely combining sharpness of wit and tenderness of heart, extremely effeminate, with deep powers of creation that were never fulfilled. His wit and his fantasy have both strongly influenced the texture of my free imagination."

15. Draine interview, 10.

16. Cf. Bernard Bergonzi, review in *Times* (London) *Literary Supplement*, 11 July 1980.

Chapter Eight

1. Ian Scott-Kilvert, "Angus Wilson," *A Review of English Literature* 1 no. 1 (April 1960): 42.

2. Edmund Wilson, *New Yorker*, 15 April 1950.

3. Radclyffe Hall's *The Well of Loneliness* appeared in 1928; E. M. Forster's *Maurice*, written in 1914, was not published until 1971.

4. *Times* (London) *Literary Supplement*, 8 August 1952, 516.

5. With, respectively, *Lucky Jim, Lord of the Flies,* and *Under the Net.*

6. John Bowen, "British Books Round the World," *Times* (London) *Literary Supplement,* 7 August 1959.

7. James Gindin, *Postwar British Fiction: New Accents and Attitudes* (Berkeley, 1962), 164.

8. Gindin, "The Fable Begins to Break Down," *Wisconsin Studies in Contemporary Literature* 8, 1 (Winter 1967).

9. *Emile Zola* (New York, 1952), 1.

10. Wilson, *London Magazine,* October 1954. Quoted by Rubin Rabinovitz, *The Reaction against Experiment in the English Novel 1950–1960* (New York and London, 1967), 65.

11. "Mythology in John Cowper Powys's Novels," *A Review of English Literature* 4, 1 (January 1963). 9–20.

12. Robert Browning, "Bishop Blougram's Apology." line 395.

13. Millgate interview, 103.

14. Ibid., 97.

15. Ibid., 98.

16. Arthur Edelstein, "Angus Wilson: The Territory Behind," in *Contemporary British Novelists,* ed. Charles Shapiro (Carbondale and Edwardsville, Ill., 1965), 144–160.

17. Walter Allen, *Tradition and Dream* (London: Phoenix House, 1964), Penguin Edition (1965), 291.

18. G. S. Fraser, *The Modern Writer and His World,* 155.

19. Ibid., 154.

20. Ian Scott-Kilvert, "Angus Wilson," 52.

21. Anthony Burgess, "Powers That Be," *Encounter* 24, 1 (January 1965): 1976.

22. Letter from Wilson to Rubin Rabinovitz, quoted in Rabinovitz, *Reaction*, 66–67.

23. Cf. *Emile Zola,* 84.

24. This is also, I feel, shown in Wilson's answers in interviews, which are quick to pick up the tone of the questions asked, and the prevailing literary fashions they imply.

25. Were the hysterical elements in Alexandra Grant influenced by the title-character of Elizabeth Bowen's novel *Eva Trout* (1969), described by her author as a "lunatic giant in the drawing-room"?

26. A. S. Byatt, "People in Paper Houses: Attitudes to 'Realism' and 'Experiment' in English Postwar Fiction," in *The Contemporary English Novel,* Stratford-Upon-Avon Studies 18 (London: Edward Arnold,1979), 24–37.

27. Malcolm Bradbury, *Possibilities: Essays in the State of the Novel* (London: Oxford University Press, 1973), 212–13.

28. Valerie A. Shaw, *The Middle Age of Mrs. Eliot* and *Late Call*: Angus Wilson's Traditionalism," *Critical Quarterly* 12, 1 (Spring 1970). 25.

29. Jonathan Raban, "Profile of Angus Wilson," *New Review* 1, 1 (April 1974): 22.

30. Draine interview, 12–14.

31. Raban, "Profile," 22.

32. Shaw, *"The Middle Age of Mrs. Eliot."* 26.

33. Raban, "Profile," 24.

Selected Bibliography

PRIMARY SOURCES

1. Novels

Hemlock and After. London: Secker & Warburg; New York: Viking Press, 1952.

Anglo-Saxon Attitudes. London: Secker & Warburg; New York: Viking Press, 1956.

The Middle Age of Mrs. Eliot. London: Secker & Warburg, 1958; New York, Viking Press, 1959.

The Old Men at the Zoo. London: Secker & Warburg; New York: Viking Press, 1961.

Late Call. London: Secker & Warburg; New York: Viking Press, 1964.

No Laughing Matter. London: Secker & Warburg; New York: Viking Press, 1967.

As If by Magic. London: Secker & Warburg; New York: Viking Press, 1973.

Setting the World on Fire. London: Secker & Warburg; New York: Viking Press, 1980.

2. Short Stories

The Wrong Set. London: Secker & Warburg; New York, William Morrow & Co., 1949. (U. S. edition includes "Totentanz.")

Such Darling Dodos. London: Secker & Warburg, 1950; New York: William Morrow & Co., 1951.

A Bit off the Map. London: Secker & Warburg; New York: Viking Press, 1957.

Death-dance: Twenty Five Stories. New York: Viking Press, 1969.

3. Plays

The Mulberry Bush. London: Secker & Warburg, 1956. "Skeletons and Assegais." *Transatlantic Review* 9 (Spring 1962). 19–43.

4. Criticism

Emile Zola: An Introductory Study of His Novels. London: Secker & Warburg; New York: William Morrow & Co., 1952.

"Diversity and Depth." *Times* (London) *Literary Supplement* 57 (15 August 1958): viii.

"The Novelist and the Narrator." *English Studies Today.* Edited by G. A. Bonnard. Berne: Francke Verlag (1961), 43–50.

"Evil in the English Novel." *Listener* 68 (27 December 1962): 1079–80; 69 (3 January 1963): 15–16; 69 (10 January 1963): 63–65; 69 (17 January 1963): 115–17.

"Mythology in John Cowper Powys's Novels." *A Review of English Literature* 4 (January 1963): 9–20.

The Wild Garden, or Speaking of Writing. London: Secker & Warburg; Berkeley and Los Angeles: University of California Press, 1963.

Tempo: The Impact of Television on the Arts. London: Studio Vista Books, 1964.

"The Artist as Your Enemy is your Only Friend." *Southern Review* 2, 2 (1966): 101–114.

The World of Charles Dickens. London: Secker & Warburg; New York: Viking Press, 1970.

"Dickens and Dostoevsky." *The Dickensian* (September 1970), 41–60.

The Strange Ride of Rudyard Kipling. London: Secker & Warburg; New York: Viking Press, 1977.

5. Miscellaneous

For Whom the Cloche Tolls: A Scrap-Book of the Twenties. Illustrated by Philippe Jullian. London: Secker & Warburg, 1953; New York: British Book Centre, 1954.

"Bexhill and After." *Spectator,* 9 May 1958.

"My Husband is Right" [Prologue to the unfinished novel, "Goat and Compasses".] *Texas Quarterly* 4 (Autumn 1961).

Introduction (7–43) to *England.* Photographs by Edwin Smith. London: Thames & Hudson, 1971.

Diversity and Depth in Fiction: Selected Critical Writings of Angus Wilson. Edited by Kerry McSweeney. London: Secker & Warburg, 1983.

SECONDARY SOURCES

1. Checklists

Escudie, Danielle. Useful list of periodical articles and reviews by Angus Wilson, in *Deux Aspects de l'Alienation dans le Roman Anglais Contemporain 1945–1965: Angus Wilson et William Golding.* Paris: Didier (Etudes Anglaises 58), 1975, 520–27.

McDowell, Frederick P. W. and Sharon E. Graves. *The Angus Wilson Manuscripts in the University of Iowa Libraries.* Iowa City: Friends of the University of Iowa Libraries, 1969.

Rabinovitz, Rubin. Bibliography of works by and about Angus Wilson, in *The Reaction against Experiment in the English Novel, 1950–1960.* New York and London: Columbia University Press, 1967, 184–95.

2. Interviews and Conversations

Barfoot, C. C. "Interview with Angus Wilson." *Dutch Quarterly Review* 6, 4 (27 February 1976): 279–90.

Biles, Jack. "An Interview in London with Angus Wilson." *Studies in the Novel* 2 (North Texas State University), Spring 1970: 76–87.

Draine, Betsy. "An Interview with Angus Wilson" (3 November 1978). *Contemporary Literature* 21, 1 (Spring 1980). 1–14.

Kermode, Frank. Interview in the Series "Myth, Reality and Fiction." *Listener* 68 (30 August 1962): 311–13. (Also printed in *Partisan Review* 30, 1 (Spring 1963): 68–71)

McDowell, Frederick P. W. "An Interview with Angus Wilson." *Iowa Review* 3, 4 (Fall, 1972): 77–105.

Millgate, Michael. "The Art of Fiction XX—Angus Wilson." *Paris Review* 17 (Autumn-Winter 1957): 89–105. Reprinted in *Paris Review Interviews,* edited by Malcolm Cowley. New York: Viking Press, 1959, 251–66.

Moorcock, Michael. "Angus Wilson talks to Michael Moorcock." *Books and Bookmen* 18, 8 (May 1973): 22–28.

Poston, Lawrence. "A Conversation with Angus Wilson." *Books Abroad* 40 (Winter 1966): 29–31.

Raban, Jonathan. "Profile of Angus Wilson." *New Review* 1, 1 (April 1974): 16–24.

3. Books, Chapters and Articles on Wilson

Bergonzi, Bernard. Section 1 of Chapter 6 ("Between Nostalgia and Nightmare"), in *The Situation of the Novel.* London: Macmillan, 1970 (Pelican Books, 1972, 177–189). Searching and perceptive commentary on Wilson's novels up to *No Laughing Matter*; particularly appreciative of *Late Call,* "arguably his most achieved work of fictional art."

Bradbury, Malcolm. "The Short Stories of Angus Wilson." *Studies in Short Fiction* 3 (Winter 1966): 117–25. Recognizes the ambiguity, the mixture of irony and sympathy, in Wilson's presentation of his characters.

――――― ."The Fiction of Pastiche: The Comic Mode of Angus Wilson", in *Possibilities.* London: Oxford University Press, 1973, 211–30. An inquiry, using *No Laughing Matter* as the (extreme) test case, into the risky coexistence in Wilson's work of "realism" and "fictiveness."

Burgess, Anthony. "Powers That Be." *Encounter* 24, 1 (January 1965): 71–76. Comparison of *Late Call* and C. P. Snow's *Corridors of Power.*

Cockshut, A. O. J. "Favoured Sons: The Moral World of Angus Wilson."

Essays in Criticism 9 (1959). 50–60. Feels that Wilson is unduly partial in his treatment of Bernard Sands, and Gerald Middleton; the reason being that, despite grave faults, they still hold up "humanism's tattered banner."

Cox, C. B. Chapter 6 ("Angus Wilson: Studies in Depression"), 117–53; and part of Chapter 7 ("Conclusion: The Modern Novel"), 154–57, in *The Free Spirit*. London and New York: Oxford University Press, 1963. Places Wilson in a line of liberal humanist writers running from George Eliot to Virginia Woolf; "rage at human inadequacy pervades his early writing," and in his work the humanist view is threatened by "breakdown and violence."

Edelstein, Arthur. "Angus Wilson: The Territory Behind," in *Contemporary British Novelists,* edited by Charles Shapiro. Carbondale and Edwardsville: Southern Illinois University Press, 1965, 144–61. A shrewd study, concentrating on *Late Call* (Wilson's "best" novel, but "disappointing"), *Anglo-Saxon Attitudes* (his "most fully achieved" novel) and *The Middle Age of Mrs. Eliot* ("a tour de force with insufficient force").

Escudie, Danielle. *Deux Aspects de l'Alienation dans le Roman Anglais Contemporain 1945–1965: Angus Wilson et William Golding.* Paris: Didier, 1975 (Etudes Anglaises 58), esp. 84–260. Detailed analysis of Wilson's first five novels, which present man as an "alienated being" needing to reconcile his urge to self-fulfillment with his wish to be integrated in society.

Faulkner, Peter. *Angus Wilson: Mimic and Moralist.* London: Secker & Warburg, 1980. Lively and often perceptive study of all Wilson's work except *Setting the World on Fire.* The strictly chronological presentation makes no distinctions of genre; but Wilson's novels are frequently illuminated by being juxtaposed to his lectures and broadcasts of the same period.

Gindin, James. "Angus Wilson's Qualified Nationalism," in *Post-War British Fiction: New Accents and Attitudes.* Berkeley: University of California Press, 1962, 145–64. Crisp overview, spoilt by occasional inaccuracies of detail; sees Wilson as "the best contemporary English novelist."

———. "The Fable Begins to Break Down." *Wisconsin Studies in Contemporary Literature* 8, 1 (Winter 1967): 1–18. Comparison of the realistic and fabular modes of fiction, partly in terms of *Late Call* and *The Old Men at the Zoo*, to the advantage of the former; Wilson still seen as "the best novelist writing in England today."

Gransden, K. W. *Angus Wilson.* London: Longmans, Green for The British Council, 1969. "Writers and Their Work" series. Shrewd essay, especially responsive to the "social documentary" aspects of Wilson; doubtful about the value of *The Middle Age of Mrs. Eliot.*

Halio, Jay L. *Angus Wilson.* Edinburgh: Oliver & Boyd, 1964. "Writers and Critics" series. First study of all Wilson's work (i.e., up to *The Old Men at the Zoo*), including useful chapters on his criticism and his plays (two of these for television and radio).

McEwan, Neil. Chapter 4 ("Angus Wilson and *No Laughing Matter*") of *The Survival of the Novel*. Totowa, New Jersey: Barnes & Noble, 1981, 60–77. Appreciative essay, stressing the novel's entertainingness and its sense of historical continuity.

Rabinovitz, Rubin. Chapter 3 of *The Reaction against Experiment in the English Novel 1950–1960*. New York and London: Columbia University Press, 1967, 64–96. Discusses Wilson's fiction up to *Late Call*; also his attitudes to fiction, which are traditional and nonexperimental while being tolerant of experiment in the work of others.

Riddell, Edwin. "The Humanist Character in Angus Wilson." *English* 21 (1972), 45–53. Sees the "central concern of Wilson's mature work" as the attempt to relate liberal attitudes to "a world largely hostile to liberalism."

Scott-Kilvert, Ian. "Angus Wilson," *A Review of English Literature* 1, 2 (April 1960): 42–53. Charts Wilson's movement from the "satire" of the short stories to the "growing human charity" of *The Middle Age of Mrs. Eliot*.

Servotte, Herman. "A Note on the Formal Characteristics of Angus Wilson's *No Laughing Matter*." *English Studies* 1, 1 (February 1969): 58–64. Sensible and perceptive commentary on the interaction of traditional narrative and fictive devices, so that reality is both presented and queried.

Shaw, Valerie A. "*The Middle Age of Mrs. Eliot* and *Late Call*: Angus Wilson's Traditionalism." *Critical Quarterly* 12, 1 (Spring 1970): 9–27. Dismisses the early view of Wilson as hostile to people; instead, emphasizes his "deep compassion for humanity." Sensitive reading of *Late Call*, which (unusually) picks up the irony intended by Wilson in "The Old Woman's Story."

Sudrann, Jean. "The Lion and the Unicorn: Angus Wilson's Triumphant Tragedy." *Studies in the Novel* 3 (Winter 1971): 390–400. A presentation of the multifaceted technique used in *No Laughing Matter* both to render human and historical meaning and to create it.

Wogatzky, Karin. *Angus Wilson's "Hemlock and After": A Study in Ambiguity*. Berne, Francke Verlag, 1971. Laborious, over-detailed analysis of a single novel, with occasional useful insights.

Index

Allen, Walter, 121
Amis, Kingsley, 14, 35, 36, 59, 119
Auden, W. H., 103
Austen, Jane, 26, 54, 68, 74, 121

Bergonzi, Bernard, 100
Betjeman, John, 110
Bexhill, 3, 27
Bowen, Elizabeth, 13, 132
Bowle, John Edward, 7
Bowra, Maurice, 7
Bradbury, Malcolm, 123
Bradfield St. George, 2, 11
Braine, John, 35, 36
British Empire Exhibitions, 6
Burgess, Anthony, 122, 124

Café Royal, 7, 63
Cary, Joyce, 46
Costley-White, Harold, 6

Death of a Salesman (Arthur Miller), 90
Dickens, 60, 61, 103, 105, 119, 120
Dostoevsky, Fyodor, 24, 25, 105, 107
Douglas, Lord Alfred, 8
Durrell, Lawrence, 119

East Anglia, University of, 11
Eliot, George, 68, 69, 121
Elizabethan, The, 1

Faulkner, Peter, 1
Forster, E. M., 26, 35, 38, 76, 105, 121
Fraser, G. S., 59, 121

Gentlemen Prefer Blonds (Anita Loos), 54
Gide, André, 38
Gransden, K. W., 36, 44
Green, Martin, 69
Golding, William, 37, 119, 121, 122, 124

Halio, Jay L., 16, 121
Hartley, L. P., 84, 94
Horizon, 1
Housman, A. E., 61
Huxley, Aldous, 7, 19, 96

Ibsen, Henrik, 24, 40, 53, 116

James, Henry, 38, 68, 121
Joyce, James, 94, 95, 119

Lawrence, D. H., 46, 103, 106

Mercer, June F., 14–15
Murdoch, Iris, 119, 124, 128

Orwell, George, 75, 84
Osborne, John, 35, 36, 51, 91, 93

Powys, J. C., 46, 120
Priestley, J. B., 51, 127
Proust, Marcel, 60, 121

Raban, Jonathan, 103, 104, 124
Rees, Goronwy, 68
Romantic Egoists, The (Louis Auchincloss), 13

Scarlet Pimpernel, The (Baroness Orczy), 5
Scott-Kilvert, Ian, 118, 121
Shaw, Valerie, 123
Sillitoe, Alan, 35, 36, 119
Sparrow, John, 7
Snow, C. P., 36, 119, 122
Socrates, 36, 38, 39, 42
Summer Before the Dark, The (Doris Lessing), 69

Tanner, Laurie, 7
That Hideous Strength (C. S. Lewis), 84

Tolkien, J. R. R., 103, 106
Trollope, Anthony, 68, 119

Victim (film), 44

Wain, John, 35, 36, 75, 119
Walker, Daniel Pickering, 8
Wall, Stephen, 38, 87
Waugh, Evelyn, 7, 32, 36–37, 84, 93, 121
Who's Who, 1
Widow, The (Francis King), 69
Wilson, Angus, early life and parentage, 3–5; in South Africa, 5; at preparatory school, 5; at Westminster School, 6–8; at Oxford, 8–9; at British Museum, 9, 10, 11, 36; war service at Bletchley Park, 9–10, 31, 87; since World War II, 11, 29; knighthood, 2, 118

WORKS:
"A Bit off the Map," 54–55
A Bit off the Map, 51–56, 69
"After the Show," 53, 112
Anglo-Saxon Attitudes, 17, 51, 53, 56–67, 71, 77, 78, 84, 86, 105, 110, 112, 121
As If By Magic, 6, 102–109, 110, 122, 123
"Christmas Day in the Workhouse," 10, 31, 87
"Crazy Crowd," 1, 15, 21
"Et Dona Ferentes," 24–26, 34
"Evil in the English Novel," 76, 87
"Flat Country Christmas, A," 51–52, 87
For Whom the Cloche Tolls, 46, 96
"Fresh-Air Fiend," 17–18, 77
"Goat and Compasses," 76, 86
"Heart of Elm," 31, 34
Hemlock and After, 17, 35, 36–46, 47, 48, 50, 58, 66, 67, 70, 76, 78, 83, 95, 106, 112, 118, 123
"Higher Standards," 52
Late Call, 4, 9, 86–94, 95, 97, 121, 122
"Learning's Little Tribute," 31, 34
"Little Companion, A," 27, 31, 34

"Live and Let Die," 56
Middle Age of Mrs. Eliot, The, 1, 57, 67–74, 75, 78, 87, 99, 110, 112
"More Friend than Lodger," 53–54
"Mother's Sense of Fun," 1, 19, 21
Mulberry Bush, The, 46–51, 83
"Mummy to the Rescue," 12, 27, 31
"Necessity's Child," 3, 12, 27, 54
"No Future for Our Young," 56
No Laughing Matter, 2, 78, 94–101, 102, 112, 113, 122, 123
Old Men at the Zoo, The, 2, 75–85, 86, 99, 105, 109, 119, 121, 122
"Once a Lady," 52
"Raspberry Jam," 1, 12, 21–23, 27
"Realpolitik," 1, 17
"Rex Imperator," 27
"Sad Fall, A," 52–53
"Saturnalia," 15–16, 42
Setting the World on Fire, 2, 7, 53, 109–17, 118, 121, 123, 131
"Significant Experience," 8, 19
"Sister Superior," 27
Skeletons and Assegais, 99
"Story of Historical Interest, A," 6, 9, 19–21
"Such Darling Dodos," 28–31, 34, 36
Such Darling Dodos, 3, 8, 12, 14, 26–33
"Ten Minutes to Twelve," 55, 112
"Totentanz," 31–33, 34, 42
"Union Reunion," 5, 18–19, 34
"Visit in Bad Taste, A," 23–24
"What Do Hippos Eat," 27–28, 78
Wild Garden, The, 2, 4, 10, 11, 29, 37, 69, 77, 119, 131
"Wrong Set, The," 16–17, 21, 27, 53
Wrong Set, The, 1, 11, 12, 13–26

Wilson, Edmund, 118
Wilson, Maude (Caney), 4; death of, 6
Wilson, William Johnstone-, 4, 27, 90, 99; death of, 9
Woolf, Virginia, 18, 19, 25, 35, 47, 61, 71, 94, 95, 119, 121

Zola, Emile, 38, 119, 127